Fostering Faith

Fostering Faith

Teaching & Learning
in the Christian Church

Denise Janssen

with Diane Janssen Hemmen and Sallie Verner

Foreword by Israel Galindo
Afterword by Margaret Ann Crain

JUDSON PRESS
PUBLISHERS SINCE 1824

Join our mailing list for updates and special offers.
www.judsonpress.com/mailing_list.cfm

Fostering Faith: Teaching & Learning in the Christian Church
© 2014 by Judson Press, Valley Forge, PA 19482-0851

Judson Press has made every effort to trace the ownership of all quotes. In the event of a question arising from the use of a quote, we regret any error made and will be pleased to make the necessary correction in future printings and editions of this book.

Unless otherwise indicated, Bible quotations in this volume are from the New Revised Standard Version of the Bible, copyright 1989, by the Division of Christian Education of the National Council of the Churches of Christ in the U.S.A. Used by permission. All rights reserved.

Cover and interior designed by Wendy Ronga / Hampton Design Group
www.hamptondesigngroup.com

Library of Congress Cataloging-in-Publication data
Janssen, Denise.
Fostering faith: teaching & learning in the Christian church/Denise Janssen, with Diane Janssen Hemmen and Sallie Verner. – first [edition]. pages cm
ISBN 978-0-8170-1749-1 (pbk.: alk. paper) 1. Sunday school teachers–Recruiting. I. Title. BV1536.5.J36 2014
268'.3–dc23   2014008419

Printed in the U.S.A.
First printing, 2014.

Contents

FOREWORD

It remains indisputably true that the task of making disciples remains one of the primary purposes of the church. Arguably, it is the church's *primary* purpose, for what else is the ultimate goal of evangelizing than to make disciples? Throughout its history, the church has answered this calling by engaging in education that is uniquely Christian. Meaning, we have practiced ways of teaching and learning that are authentically Christian. This is easier said than done. It is not difficult to acquire effective ways of teaching and learning. We can rely on vast resources from the field of education and all its domains: pedagogy, andragogy, developmental psychology, instructional design, adult education, and the plethora of emerging instructional technologies. The challenge for congregations, however, is to answer the question, "What ways of teaching and learning are authentically Christian?"

Traditional congregational Christian education has seen noticeable decline in the past decades. As congregations get smaller (75 is the average worship attendance in congregations today), as fewer professional Christian educators find places of ministry in congregations, and as seminaries scale back their Christian education degree programs, the consequences to the church are on the cusp of being tragic.

One renowned educator wrote,

> In modern times people's views about education differ. There is no general agreement about what the young should learn either in relation to moral virtue or to success in life; nor is it clear whether education should be more concerned with training the intellect or the character. Contemporary events have made the problem more difficult, and there is no certainty

whether education should be primarily vocational, moral or cultural. People have advocated all three. Moreover there is no agreement as to what sort of education promotes moral virtue.

The author of that observation was Aristotle (in *Politics VII*), which goes to prove the biblical adage: there is nothing new under the sun.

We may think it quaint that Aristotle situated his comment in "modern times." He was, however, addressing the same questions of concern to today's Christian educators, namely, the perennial questions about the nature of education, learning, and teaching, and questions about the nature of the teacher and of the learner.

Aristotle's observation can help us appreciate that these perennial questions of education must be addressed perennially. But they need to be dealt with responsibly and critically if we are ever to figure out what it's all about: what should be the goal of Christian education? What methods and approaches are appropriate to that end? What is the nature of the Christian learner? Of the Christian teacher? What should comprise the content of the curriculum (explicit, implicit, and null)? What is worth knowing, and what is trivial? How do students learn, and how do you know? And more important for us, "What are authentic ways to teach Christian education authentically?"

While it may be true that traditional congregational education has had a rough patch of late, as so often is the case, at the same time there is evidence of a resurgence in the felt need for effective congregational Christian education. In this work, Janssen, Hemmen, and Verner strike all the right chords for an approach to effective Christian education in the local church, one that can help congregational Christian educators, clergy and lay. Their emphases include:

■ Attention to the context of the congregation for faith education
■ Appreciation for effective teaching and learning practices that are educationally sound

■ The necessity of developing the office of teaching: calling, giftedness, nurture, and cultivating appreciation

■ The importance of educational administration in the church: organization, leadership, oversight, and planning

This new resource, *Fostering Faith: Teaching & Learning in the Christian Church*, provides a strong introduction to the work and calling of congregational Christian education. It is a helpful guide to answering the question of how to provide a Christian education that is authentically Christian.

—Israel Galindo
Associate Dean, Lifelong Learning
Columbia Theological Seminary

How to Use This Book

In American culture, we have a penchant for going places—and a strong desire to get there fast. We just love to hop in the car (or on a plane, train, or bus) and go where we want to go at a particular time. You may have picked up this book hoping to do just that: get to where you want to be with regard to Christian education in your setting, and get there fast—like right now!

In that regard, we have some very good news and maybe also some less-than-good news. The good news is that this is a resource carefully assembled with a wealth of ideas and tools that will be helpful to you and your congregation as together you seek to strengthen the vital role teachers play in your church. The less-than-good news is that this book may not do everything you'd like it to do—answer every question you have and provide every resource you need—as perfectly as you'd hoped. However, this book will provide you with some tools to help you figure out where to start and to discern what parts will be most helpful to you and your congregation right away.

Close your eyes for a moment and imagine this book is like a traffic circle, a roundabout. Each vehicle in a traffic circle enters at one of several places. The vehicle then continues around the circle until it reaches an exit that will take it in the direction it needs to go. Sometimes, when drivers aren't sure of their routes, they will go around the traffic circle a couple of times, watching for the right exit. And sometimes, on another day and coming from another direction, drivers may reenter the traffic circle looking for a different exit. Similarly, you may come to this book today with a particular question or set of issues you're addressing.

You'll find some ideas and resources to help by heading off in a particular direction. But later in the year, you may come again to this resource with another set of questions. Around the traffic circle you'll go again, this time taking a different exit in the direction of another set of helpful ideas and resources. This is a book to keep handy, in the glove box, if you will, to help you work with others to strengthen your congregation's Christian education programs.

The appendices contain a couple of basic tools to aid in navigating this book. They are designed to help you figure out where to begin and where to go next. They will also help you understand your own context and the ways the ideas included here can be adapted to meet your particular needs.

If you're in a hurry or have particular issues that led you to pick up this book, you may want to begin with the "Triage Worksheet" in appendix A. It will help you identify a starting place or several options for where you might begin to use this book. "The Know Your Context Worksheet" in appendix B will help you identify some of your congregation's existing commitments with regard to faith formation. Knowing your context and becoming clearer about these existing commitments will be helpful as you work toward a healthier and stronger Christian education program.

You can, of course, just begin at the beginning of this book. To quote a familiar lyric from *The Sound of Music*, the beginning *is* "a very good place to start"! But even if you are able to work through this book yourself or with a group in the order it is offered, you still may want to revisit particular sections for ideas as issues arise.

However you choose to use this book, the authors pray that it will be helpful to you and inspire you in the important ministry of Christian education.

INTRODUCTION

Denise Janssen

If you want to build a ship, don't herd people together to collect wood, and don't assign them tasks and work, but rather
teach them to long for the endless immensity of the sea.
—Antoine de Saint-Exupéry

When I think back on the impact teachers had in my life, the ones who
transformed my faith were the ones who were themselves deeply in
love with God. It was, in fact, their love for God and their passion for
doing God's work in the world that were irresistibly compelling to me.
As a professor of Christian education at the graduate level, I realize that
they probably also employed effective educational strategies, understood something about multiple intelligences and age-level characteristics, and worked hard to tailor the printed resources to the needs of the
particular learners with whom they were working. But it is also clear to
me, from an educational standpoint, that formation in faith is something that cannot be taught with effectiveness by one who has not been
formed in faith and continually transformed by it himself or herself.[1]

Thus, prior to exploring the plethora of other ideas and strategies
contained in this book, the best preparation or the most useful tool a
teacher in the church can have is a vital faith. Knowing about God or
understanding teaching and learning strategies is no substitute for faithful discipleship in the lives of teachers in the church. Vital faith, evi-
denced by love of God and neighbor in tangible ways, should be the
base level for every teacher in the church.

Before moving on, I believe we should be clear about one other thing: people are motivated to accept a role as a teacher in the church, and continue in such a role, for a wide variety of reasons. Not every one of those reasons is charitable; in fact, some can be self-serving. And rarely are people clear about their motivations to teach or continue to teach.

The vast majority of people who accept an invitation to teach in the church do so with the best of intentions and motivations. Perhaps they want to help their peers grow in faith as they themselves have, or maybe they are inspired by the eagerness and honesty of children, for example. They may want to share their faith with the next generation, just as their forebears did for them. People who are motivated to teach often need to be equipped for this important role and provided with supplemental resources, support, inspiration, and affirmation. But the single most important criteria for teachers is a vital life of faith.

The epigraph at the beginning of this chapter is enlightening both for how we might think about equipping teachers for their role and also for how teachers reflect on their work: "If you want to build a ship, don't herd people together to collect wood, and don't assign them tasks and work, but rather teach them to long for the endless immensity of the sea." Really effective, inspired teaching is not so much something that can be taught in a how-to or mechanistic fashion—although aspects of the art of teaching could be shared in this way. Enthusiastic, influential teaching has at its core a desire to share the good news of God's grace and love for all people, indeed for all creation. Moved by the grace and love of God in their own lives, the best teachers are compelled to share that love and grace with others. Those who "long for the endless immensity of the sea"—and teachers who are motivated by a deep love for God and for God's children (of all ages!)—feel differently about the toil and tasks. When one is doing what one loves, it hardly seems like work at all, and going the extra mile becomes almost effortless.

If we heed the advice of Antoine de Saint-Exupéry, a desire to teach and an understanding of the art of teaching may also be something inspired by experiencing the joy of participating in the learning of others. Learning with a creative teacher who is passionate about his or her faith can inspire us to become passionate and creative teachers ourselves, simply through seeing and experiencing the effects of such teaching in our own lives. Further, coming into contact with someone whose love of God is contagious, someone whose thinking about faith is integrated with living that faith every day, can be far more inspiring and compelling than being instructed in a list of dos and don'ts or a litany of good educational practices.

What's the Point of Christian Education in the Church?

What's the point of Christian education in the church? This is a question we need to get clear about right from the start as we seek to create or strengthen Christian education programs in our congregations. If we aren't clear about the results we're hoping for, we can't be sure what steps to take or not to take, and we can't tell if the results we got are the ones we wanted.

Christian education that moves toward transformation of learners in life-giving ways involves creating a hospitable environment for learners to encounter God, and to practice discerning God's presence in their lives and in the world. To practice discerning God's presence necessarily requires that we make meaning of those experiences. When learners come together, as they do in study groups or church school classes, they consider their meanings in light of Scripture and the church's teachings about God throughout their lives. In so doing, those learners are sometimes confronted with new meanings and experiences of others. When laid alongside the meanings learners have assigned to their experiences with God throughout their own lives, the new meanings and experiences of others call individual learners to reinterpret or transform their current understandings, beliefs, and meanings. "New experiences may call us into transforming both our personal meanings and those of the tradition."[2] Encountering new ideas and experiences almost inescapably brings about transformation in learners—or at least that's the hope. Understanding transformation as the hoped-for result of Christian education enlightens our process toward it.

So What's at Stake Here?

Let's be frank: if we were referring with this book to just the one or two hours each week that most congregations list in their calendars for formal educational activities, it wouldn't much matter how such Christian education was carried out. But if we understand education in the church more broadly as all those activities that form us in the faith, then we begin to understand that everything and everyone in the congregation teaches. The ideas in this book go far beyond the Sunday school hour or Wednesday evening study groups. They have implications for the whole life of the congregation. (More about that in chapter 1.)

For now, I invite you to listen for the wind and smell the salt air and feel the spray on your face. Be reminded of the passionate and creative faith of those with whom you've been building this ship. Be inspired by the "endless immensity of the sea" that makes your heart sing and calls to you with the voice that first stirred in your heart the love of our awesome God. Dream dreams and see visions, and let your heart long for the one who called it into being.

Notes

1. For more on this idea, see Parker J. Palmer, *The Courage to Teach: Exploring the Inner Landscape of a Teacher's Life* (San Francisco: Wiley & Sons, 2007).

2. Jack L. Seymour, Margaret Ann Crain, and Joseph V. Crockett, *Educating Christians: The Intersection of Meaning, Learning, and Vocation* (Nashville: Abingdon, 1993), 94–95.

CHAPTER ONE

Why Teach?

Denise Janssen

> But we have this treasure in clay jars, so that it may be made
> clear that this extraordinary power belongs to God and does
> not come from us.
> —2 Corinthians 4:7

Why teach? To change the world, in partnership with God! I recognize
that's a bold statement, so let's take some time to look more carefully at
why we believe teaching and learning is important in forming faithful
followers of Christ—important enough to make such a bold claim.

Why Teach?

If we're truthful, likely many of us involved in the educational ministry
of the church give the question "Why teach?" very little conscious consideration. Much of the time, our local congregations do what we have
always done. We start the Sunday school year in September when children go back to school because that's when we always do it. Our congregation's primary Christian education time takes place on the same
day and at the same time it always has—and we rail at the soccer games
that draw children and families away. We group adults in certain ways
for classes, and we don't really ask why. Children's classes are grouped
by grade because it's what we remember doing in our childhood. The

1

youth class meets in a room with broken and worn-out couches and chairs thrown away or donated by church members because we assume that's what will make teenagers feel comfortable. Really, we don't often stop to consider why we do what we are doing, particularly if we were "cradle Christians" and the church has always been part of our lives.

Now, just because we haven't carefully considered all the aspects of our church's educational ministry, at least not on a conscious level, that doesn't mean teaching and learning in our congregation is unimportant or doomed to be ineffective. I believe the work of educating and equipping people for lives of faithful discipleship and service is the most important work the church does! And if we take some time to consider why we teach, I believe we'll be even more enthused about our roles in this life-changing ministry.

Because It's Our Shared Responsibility as the Body of Christ

Maria Harris, in her very helpful work *Fashion Me a People*, observes that the focus or purpose of education in the church has been changing, along with the primary model. Formerly, an individual (often a church leader like the pastor or another staff person) was responsible for instructing children to know the stories of the faith and indoctrinating them to affirm a particular set of beliefs. But, Harris observes, a shift began taking place in the twentieth century. The agent of the church's education, the responsible person, was no longer understood to be primarily the pastor or another church official. Rather, educating in the faith has come to be understood as the work of the whole community of faith, empowering the whole community to engage their vocations in ministry with the world around them. Further, the idea that children were the primary focus of teaching and learning in the church was no longer dominant. Lifelong learning in faith, particularly in Protestant circles, became more prevalent.

This shift in thinking about education in the church is important for our purposes as we consider this chapter's focus: "Why teach?"

As is the case in other forms of education, the church's primary model of education has been shifting. It is shifting from education as "schooling," with a goal to increase learners' knowledge, to a model of education as transformation, to equip and empower Christian disciples for ministry. The shift away from near-exclusive use of a schooling model has meant a broader scope of activities and settings for learning, and a more synergistic understanding of the relationships within the classroom. Along with the explosion of information, first in book form and now readily available electronically, has come an understanding of education as something lifelong rather than a set course of topics to be mastered in order to be declared "educated" or "graduated."[1]

Because People Want to Make Meaning of Their World
Congregations and individuals are becoming increasingly comfortable with the postmodern notion that *learning the answers* is less the goal of education than *discerning the questions* and learning how to address them and live with them. Figuring out and living with questions, and equipping those who journey with us to do so, requires a vastly different set of tools than the schooling model that our past required.

Educating people for a faith that focuses more on questions than answers involves different learning experiences and contexts, as well as a lifelong term to be accomplished. If we expect, as a growing number of congregations do, that people all through life have questions, needs, and hopes that can be met by the gospel, then it makes sense that the scope of education in the congregation will have to expand to meet these growing expectations.

Because We Each Are Already Teaching All the Time
As I have already said, the ideas in this book go far beyond the Sunday school hour or Wednesday evening Bible study. They have implications for the whole life of the congregation. The ideas in this book are relevant far beyond those invited into formal teaching

positions. The entire course of the church's life, Maria Harris observes, is relevant to fashioning people in faith.[2] When we begin to realize that everything, everyone, every moment teaches *something*, then equipping the congregation for its teaching ministry becomes a much larger job.

Most of us have heard the old adage "Actions speak louder than words." This statement is true in our lives of faith and, in particular, in teaching. Its corollary, "Words speak, too, both in what we say and what we leave out," is also true in the teaching ministry of the church. Keeping these in mind and holding them in tension reminds us of what is at stake when we begin to consider teaching and learning in the life of the congregation.

Our teaching may be explicit and intentional, for example, as exemplified by the Bible lessons in Sunday school. Our teaching might also be implied by the manner in which we act or speak. Our tone or facial expressions can convey a message that might just counteract the words we use—that's "implied" teaching. Another way we teach is by who is included in decision making. We even teach something very important by what we leave out—what topics are not discussed, whose opinions and voices are not present, what questions are not welcomed. We teach all the time—at business meetings, at coffee hour, by how we relate to one another, by how we care for our spaces, by who gets priority or whose opinion matters most.[3]

If it is true that congregations teach all the time, then the whole church must accept responsibility for the teaching and learning that takes place, and become more intentional about faithfully equipping the faithful to live out their faith in the world. From the pastor to the lay leadership of boards and committees to the women's and men's groups, from the musicians to the ushers and greeters to the youth and children—no one is exempt from teaching and learning, and no one is excused from a responsibility for both teaching and learning.

Teaching for Transformation

That brings us back one more time to the question "Why teach?" Let me respond with something that has inspired my teaching, something that became clearer through these ideas I first heard shared by my friend and mentor Jack Seymour, professor of religious education at Garrett-Evangelical Theological Seminary.

My upbringing in faith made it easy for me to think of the food laws from the Hebrew Scriptures as some kind of arcane legalism, a relic that no longer served much purpose. Then one day Jack talked about the deeper effect the practice of observing kosher food laws served in forming identity and faith in the Jewish faith. For one who observes kosher food laws, identity as a Jew is constantly in view. One cannot eat or think about eating, cook, shop for groceries, or even do dishes without remembering one's identity as a Jew. Food is everywhere in our lives, and for Jews who observe them, kosher laws serve to form them in a faith identity. Never mind the one hour of formal education in faith in many Christian churches; the laws about keeping kosher have served for many generations as an all-the-time, hands-on teaching and learning experience. Our Jewish friends and forebears in the faith teach in order to form identity in faith.

The example of our Jewish sisters and brothers in the faith is very helpful in informing our response to the question "Why teach?" The example makes me ask, what do Christians do that functions similarly? I think of things like a prayer before meals, morning devotions, and fasting as Christian practices that function in similar ways to remind us of our identity in Christ. Consider the way that, in the Last Supper, Jesus used common items that would be on almost every table nearly every day to help reinforce a faith identity in his disciples.

I'm reminded of Jesus' parables that use everyday experiences and items to teach something about what is expected of people who follow in his way. Much of the time, these experiences or items were reinterpreted by Jesus to demonstrate how faith in God calls us to see things differently than we might without the lens of faith, to respond to things differently, and to understand ourselves differently in light of God's love and grace.[4]

This is key: we teach in order to participate in the transformation of people into disciples of Jesus Christ, into bearers of the gospel in the world, and into agents of transformation themselves. The church's teaching ministry has transformation as its primary goal. Why teach? To join in Jesus' mission to change the world with God's love and grace, one person at a time.

Notes

1. Maria Harris, *Fashion Me a People: Curriculum in the Church* (Louisville: Westminster John Knox, 1989), 39, 46–47.

2. Ibid., 17.

3. For a fuller explanation of the concept of explicit, implicit, and null curriculum, see Elliot W. Eisner, *The Educational Imagination* (New York: Macmillan, 1979), 74–92.

4. To read more about how Christian practices form faith, see Craig Dykstra, *Growing in the Life of Faith: Education and Christian Practices*, 2nd ed. (Louisville: Westminster John Knox, 2005); and Dorothy C. Bass, *Practicing Our Faith: A Way of Life for a Searching People* (New York: Wiley & Sons, 2010).

CHAPTER TWO

The Invitation to Teach

Sallie Verner and Denise Janssen

> If you are a dreamer, come in. If you are a dreamer, a wisher,
> a liar, a hope-er, a pray-er, a magic bean buyer. . . . If you're a
> pretender, come sit by my fire, for we have some flax-golden
> tales to spin. Come in! Come in!
> —Shel Silverstein, *Where the Sidewalk Ends*

Invitations open the door to discovering something new about ourselves through the lens of the other. When it comes right down to it,
invitations are about relationship.

In an age when most of us rarely get "snail" mail besides bills and mar-
keting mail anymore, opening the mailbox to discover a fancy envelope
brings a sense of excitement. The envelope has the possibility of bringing with it the anticipation of time spent with friends, laughter and
smiles, good food and drink, meaningful conversation, and celebration.
Whether we are children invited to a birthday party, teenagers invited to
a dance, or adults invited to a wedding, at the most basic level, invitations
are about relationships. The recipient is invited to participate in a special
event. The person issuing the invitation is asking the recipient to join
with others who also have a relationship with the inviter.

Inviting people to be leaders and teachers in the educational programs of the church can carry this same sense of excitement, anticipation, and celebration. How people feel about being invited depends on

such details as the language and style of the invitation as well as the relationship they have with the one doing the inviting. Our invitation draws upon an invitation to relationship we have already received from God. The purpose of this invitation from God is centuries old: we are called to keep the vision of the Hebrew and Christian Scriptures alive by sharing our faith with our peers and with future generations. We are called to teach the stories of our faith as we have come to know the truth in them in our own lives.

When God Sends the Invitation

Invitations of various types appear throughout Scripture. Consider God's invitation to enter into covenant—an invitation extended to Abraham and Sarah (Genesis 15–17) and later to David (2 Samuel 7). Talk about your irresistible invitations! These covenants were one-sided contracts binding God to a set of actions that were not dependent on the responses of the other contractual party.

God was going to be Abraham and Sarah's God whether or not they followed faithfully. God was going to give them the land God promised, whether or not they responded with trust and love. Similarly, when King David announced that he was going to build God a house, God instead made King David a "house" and gave him a legacy, and this was not dependent on anything King David did. The covenant language offered a way King David might respond to God's goodness, but it was not conditional for God to do what God promised.

Invitations abound in the Gospels and Epistles as well. Consider Jesus' invitation to the people who eventually became known as his disciples: "Follow me." There must have been some sort of invitation to the wedding Jesus and his friends and family attended at Cana. Paul saw in a dream a Macedonian person inviting him to cross over and visit. And then there's the invitation Peter received in a dream to "kill and eat" when the sheet full of unclean animals was lowered before him.

Biblical invitations seem to have a few things in common: the invitation fits the persons being invited and considers their needs and gifts. Invitations are best issued in a manner that is compelling to recipients and makes them want to accept. Invitations are sometimes unexpected and not exactly what the invitees were hoping for—yet they are often just what the invitees need most. The means of invitation and the method matter, as do the inviters and the invitees.

Invitations issued also reflect how the inviters feel about the thing to which they are doing the inviting. If we feel ashamed of the thing we are inviting people to, our invitation will be apologetic. Invitations in Scripture rarely have any hint of apology. Rather, they are issued boldly and joyfully, reflecting the great value placed on the thing to which the invitation refers.

How do our invitations to leadership and service subtly telegraph how we really feel about what we are inviting people to do? How can we invite with boldness and joyfulness?

Invitation to a Unique Relationship

When we are invited to be leaders and teachers, we are invited to enter into a relationship—a relationship with other leaders and teachers and a relationship with our students. And we are invited to share the best news ever, news of God's amazing love and grace. What a fabulous gift! A gift like that should come in a really special package that reflects the amazing nature of what is inside! The way the invitation is packaged is an important key to the invitation process. It should come as elegantly presented as a wedding invitation. It should come with the balloons and ribbons and flowers we attach to birthday parties and dances. It should come with a sense of excitement and anticipation.

If you are reading this chapter, you may have accepted the responsibility (either alone or with others) for recruiting teachers and leaders in your church's educational program. Before going any further, take a moment right now and recall the most exciting invitation you have ever received. Maybe the invitation was to

- the wedding of a dear friend,
- the retirement celebration for a mentor who deeply impacted your life,
- an awards ceremony where you were honored for your achievements or outstanding service, or
- the dedication or baptismal service for your first grandchild.

Can you translate that experience to this one? Can you imagine inviting (not recruiting) members of your church to participate as leaders and teachers in the educational program? What would it take for you to bring that same sense of enthusiasm to this process? Who else do you know who shares this sense of excitement about teaching? As you work your way through the process suggested in the ten steps outlined below, we hope you will find that sense of excitement and anticipation that will enable you to invite others to join you in the celebration of sharing their faith. (These steps are also great for inviting other kinds of leaders.)

10 Steps for Inviting Teachers

1. Plan the invitation process. Begin by recalling an invitation you especially liked or appreciated, either one you received or one you sent. Spend a few minutes reflecting on (and sharing with others if you're working with a group) the details of the invitation. How did the invitation come? What did it look like? To what event were you invited (or to what event were you inviting people)? How did you feel? What did you especially like about it? Consider how you can invite in a way that reflects the uniqueness and importance of the thing to which you are inviting others. Plan the invitation process—it may have several steps.

2. Get clear about expectations—on both sides. Being clear about expectations for teachers is one of the very best ways to show you respect those whom you are inviting to teach. Be equally clear about what teachers can expect from the experience—the support provided and the benefits of the ministry. A teacher job description is a great way to address this. Prepare a job description for volunteer teachers that includes the following items.

Responsibilities. When does the teaching responsibility begin? From what start time to what end time are teachers expected to be present? What is the process for teachers who need to miss a session (find their own substitute or call someone appointed to handle this)? For what period of time are teachers accepting responsibility, and what is assumed about continuing in this role after that term? And what exactly are you inviting them to do?

Resources. What tools are provided (printed curriculum resources, basic supplies in the teaching space, technology tools or other audiovisual tools, craft supplies, snacks)? What tools are teachers expected to provide (additional teaching tools, snacks, craft supplies, technology tools)? Is reimbursement provided for tools teachers provide, and what is the process for approval of purchases and reimbursement?

Support. What training is provided on how to use the printed curriculum resources or technology tools? What continuing education is offered to help teachers learn more about teaching and increase their effectiveness? Is participation in ongoing training and support optional or required?

Benefits. Create a list of special perks that teachers can enjoy. For example, having access to good coffee prepared for them and designated for teachers only on Sunday morning; gaining possession of the supply closet key along with a list of all the supplies provided for them there; enjoying free teacher lunches once a quarter for support and training; getting hugs from adorable children; building relationships with adult learners, parents, and other volunteers; learning more as they prepare to teach; leaving a legacy in lives transformed; connecting people across generations; and so on. Consider the benefits you have experienced and enjoy most—probably these will appeal to others as well.

Step 2 calls into question the support you can promise teachers, which needs to be carefully considered. This leads us to step 3.

3. Establish support systems. The next step in the invitation process is to consider carefully what the Christian education staff person or the Christian education committee can promise to provide the teachers. You may have started thinking about this question when considering the teacher benefits to include in the job description in step 2. Ideally, support structures and personnel should be in place before teachers are invited. If a committee or team is already in place, often these are the people with responsibility for these matters, or at least some specific aspects.

The environment you provide for learning is very important. As part of considering how best to support teachers, you may want to take a field trip through each of the classrooms. Often we become so accustomed to what we see around us that we stop seeing resources and deficiencies. Put yourself in the place of a teacher or participant going into a classroom for the first time. In appendix E you will find the list "Standard Supplies Every Classroom Needs." Take the list with you on the field trip to determine what work needs to be done before the educational program begins. You might want to deliberately work through the classrooms, making improvements as you go along, or choose to set a workday for the improvement process if a classroom needs a lot of attention. Think about making improvements in stages or steps if they can't all be made at once.

The "Promises, Promises: We've Got Your Back Worksheet" (appendix F) is designed to help you think about the support provided for each teacher and by whom. Being able to say to potential teachers, "This is what we promise to have in place and provide for you if you accept this invitation" is a way of telling teachers that they are not alone, that people and resources are in place to support their teaching.

Talk through the list on the "Promises, Promises" worksheet. Make changes appropriate for your situation. Put on the list only those things that you are willing to promise and capable of fulfilling. For example, can the church afford to provide curriculum for each child? If not, what can/will you provide? Is the teacher/leader expected to make copies of handouts, color pages, and puzzles at their own expense? Will you provide supplies (basic ones as well as special supplies for specific activities)? Will someone (Sunday school superintendent, staff person, volunteer coordinator) be coming by or be available during the teaching time to gather a forgotten supply from the supply closet or to help with a crying child or a physically ill participant? Is the teacher responsible for putting up bulletin boards or decorating the meeting space (and are supplies available for it)? Is a bulletin board or tack strip available for posting participants' work or theme material related to the class topic? Is audiovisual equipment available in classroom, or does it need to be requested in advance, and is training available on how it works? What should teachers do if they are sick or have a sick child at the last minute?

Remember, when you issue an invitation, being able to say to the prospective teacher, "We will promise to have these things in place for you" is a way to say that this work is important to you. Even before teachers invest themselves in the work, you are also investing in it—and in them! Addressing such practical concerns proactively communicates that you have taken seriously what teachers will need to do the work and that you are promising to support them in a multitude of ways. Clarify the support you can offer teachers, and then set this worksheet aside for a moment.

4. Develop a list of criteria important for good teachers. Use "Teacher Qualities and Characteristics Worksheet" in appendix C to develop a list of criteria you believe to be important characteristics for teachers/leaders. Make copies of appendix C for each person on the ministry team or committee. After each person on the team has completed ranking the items with a 1 (most important), 2 (somewhat important), or 3 (not very important), share your work.

Are you in agreement? If not, you'll need to make a case for the qualities you believe are most important and negotiate. Do you have a sense of what characteristics you will look for in the people you invite to be teachers/leaders? Circle the top five qualities and characteristics you come to agree on as the most important. There may be different priorities for different age groups of participants (e.g., young children have some different needs in a teacher than do adults or youth).

Are any of these nonnegotiable? How do you handle special circumstances? What if a potential teacher is always out of town on the third Sunday of the month? What if a potential teacher specifically wants to teach with a different person or at a different age level than what you had in mind? What if a potential teacher wants to use a different printed curriculum resource than the materials recommended or selected by the committee?

Spend a few minutes talking about each of the items on the list. Which of the details are so important that a potential teacher's being unable to commit to them will lead you to thank the individual for considering the invitation and to say that you will be in touch again next year? After the conversation, make a list of the nonnegotiable items. Set it aside to use later.

5. Clarify who is inviting whom to do what and when. The answers to these questions need to be in place before an invitation can be extended. Who is issuing the invitation? To what are recipients invited? When does the activity begin? Where will attendees meet? What is the time frame? What are the expectations of guests (preparation, responsibilities, training)? The worksheet "Details, Details: Clarifying the Invitation to Teach" (appendix D) is designed to address these questions. If you are working as part of an education committee or team, work through the worksheet as a group to make sure everyone is on the same page.

6. Identify the teacher staffing needs of the congregation or program. If an acquaintance says to me that she is inviting a few friends over sometime on Tuesday, and why don't I stop by too, I may not be inclined to do so—not without more information. If, on the other hand, she gives me the specifics (for example, "I am hoping that you will come to my home for a cookie sampling party on Tuesday at 2:00 p.m. along with a small group of others from church . . ."), the invitation feels very different.

The same principle is true when inviting people to be teachers in the church. It is much easier to think about and respond to a specific request. Being told, "Hey, you ought to teach Sunday school" may be momentarily flattering, but it is too ambiguous and abstract to be inviting. To be asked to teach the kindergarten class leads me to think about kindergarten-aged children I know and to picture myself reading them a story or helping them with an activity. To be asked to coordinate a men's group each Tuesday morning at McDonald's may well make me start to think about how to mix mornings and McMuffins, faith and fellowship.

Adapt the sample "Opportunities Overview Worksheet" in appendix G for your situation. Create a chart that lists the classes and openings for the educational program for which you have accepted the responsibility of inviting teachers to participate. Include on the chart names of those teachers already in place. Also remember to include all of the positions for which invitations need to be extended.

7. Create a list of potential teachers. Gather names of those with gifts and qualities that may make them good teachers. Consider long-time members and new members, parents of young children and empty nesters, former teachers and friends of former teachers, consistent attendees and those who indicate their interest in learning and growing. Are there people from previous years who could not accept an invitation to teach at that time but wanted to be asked another year? Are there parents who always volunteer to help in the classroom who might enjoy team-teaching? This initial list should be broad. Think of it as brainstorming. Appendix H, a lighthearted piece called "You Might Be a Sunday School Teacher If . . . ," can assist you in considering the gifts and graces of those in your congregation who might be called upon to teach.

Keep in mind any policies in place about those who can teach in your church as you do this. Some congregations have a policy of inviting members to teach only after they have been members for six months, or of not having parents teach in the classroom where their own children are learners. Pay attention, too, to child and youth protection policies the congregation may have in place. (Child and youth protection policies refer to a set of guidelines a church creates and follows to protect vulnerable populations—including children, elderly, differently abled people—from abuse and harm in the context of the church's programs.) If your church doesn't have such a policy, you may want to consider creating one and following it. See appendix I for a sample policy or consult your church's insurance company.

When the list is completed, review the "Teacher Qualities and Characteristics Worksheet" (appendix C) to determine if the people on the list meet the criteria previously set out for teachers/leaders. Make a new list of the people who meet the criteria. Review each name, noting what you know about the leader/teacher. For example, if the person has a child, what age is the child? If the person has taught before, what age group did he or she teach? What special talents and gifts does the person have? (For example, do you see seventh graders talking to him at family night suppers? Is she good at organizing?) Think about partnering people intentionally. For example, do you want three new members leading the adult Bible study on Thursday evening, or could a mix of new and longer-term members make this a more rewarding experience for all?

On the "Opportunities Overview Worksheet" (appendix G), pencil in the names of potential teachers/leaders for the openings you have identified. You might choose to put a name in more than one place if you believe someone would be equally good at teaching, for example, both four-year-olds and first graders. You can finalize the assignment later. If there are more openings than names, consider combining some of the identified needs. You might, for example, ask the same person to teach both second and third graders if the total number of students allows for a combined class. Or you might ask the same person who is purchasing supplies to also be available during the class to provide support for teachers. When you are working with teaching teams, another consideration is who will work well together. Think about putting friends on the same team or putting a new member with someone you know will be welcoming to him or her. Then set the "Opportunities Overview Worksheet" aside for later.

At this point, it will be tempting to grab someone in the hall and ask them to teach the four-year-olds. It will be tempting to divide the list and start making phone calls. Don't yield to temptation! Some important decisions about what kind of invitation you want to send need to be made! Hold off for now—you will be glad you did.

8. Develop the invitation. There are a number of things to consider before deciding on the final version of the invitation. One that may be of help is the culture of your faith community. When designing the invitation, think about your congregation. Would you characterize yourselves as formal or informal? Are you fun-loving or serious? Are you urban or rural? Are you family or corporate? Are you young or old? Do you prefer programs focused outside or inside the walls? Will the lettering be blue or green? Will it come with balloons or flowers? Will it be electronic or on paper? The presentation is important. Most congregations have preferences and styles of functioning that have developed over time. Sometimes these are nothing more than bad habits and need to be changed. You need not be bound by the preferences you identify, but it helps to pay attention to them. A few minutes spent thinking about the culture of your faith community might give you some clues about the style and format of the invitation. Here are some examples of what we mean:

> An inner-city church gathered in their physical space on only two days of the week, Sunday mornings and Wednesday nights. A significant number of the members had a thirty-minute drive

from their home to the church. The church did not have a parking lot, which made it even more difficult for members to gather at the church for meetings, so meetings were often held at the homes of members. These two factors led to neighborhood teaching teams. Members who lived on the same side of the city could more easily gather for planning meetings.

Some Potential Invitation Ideas in Their Contexts

First Neighborhood Church had just completed a new educational building, which gave them the opportunity to change their Sunday morning program. The Christian education committee decided to have a "Come See Us Now" party for the potential teachers they had identified. The church school hour was the time they identified as the best time frame for having the most people in attendance. Each potential teacher received a written invitation in the mail. A follow-up phone call was made to answer questions and encourage participation. As each person entered the gathering space, they were given a special pair of glasses, like inexpensive 3-D glasses or fireworks glasses, to help them "see."

In small groups, the guests rotated through three very different visual spaces with members of the CE Committee to hear about new plans for the coming year, to learn about how teachers would be supported in their work, and to hear stories about the transformation experienced by participants in the church's education programs. Ample time was given for the guests to ask questions about the roles they were being asked to fill. A tour of the new building spaces completed the "Come See Us Now" party. Within three days, a member of the CE Committee phoned each guest to issue an invitation to become a teacher in the church school program.

Another church located in a historic community strongly identified itself with the rich history of its surroundings. The buildings were open to tour groups every day, and members of the church served as docents. Understanding this part of the church culture and the role it played in the educational programs was important to teachers and leaders. Part of the

Old St. Paul Church had developed a dedicated core of teachers for the four adult classes it offered on Sunday mornings. The classes and teachers had been in place for many years. At the February meeting of the Adult Education Committee, several members reported that they were hearing rumors that most of the teachers were planning to "retire" at the end of the summer. The committee chair assigned two people to check out the rumors and report back at the March meeting. The reports confirmed the rumors. Of the twelve teachers in place, only two planned to continue teaching. The committee decided to enlist the help of the current teachers in identifying and recruiting replacements.

After working through the "Details, Details" and "Promises, Promises" worksheets, the committee met with the current teachers to identify potential teachers. Based on committee members' and current teachers' knowledge of the potential teachers and the personalities of the current teachers and adult education members, the names were divided and each potential teacher was invited to have coffee with a current teacher and a committee member in order to issue a two-on-one invitation. The combination of a committee member who could explain the reason for the invitation and outline what the committee would do to support an incoming teacher, with a current teacher who could talk about his or her experience in the ministry, made a powerful impression on the potential teacher.

process of being invited to be a teacher was an educational event focused on the history of the community and the role the church had played in that history.

In extending the invitation to teach, you need to take into account the culture of your congregation, as well as its patterns and habits. Considering the culture of the church may have other added benefits, as well, such as bringing to mind additional kinds of teaching and learning groups you could offer or causing you to reflect on topics on which you might want to focus.

9. Design the invitation. With the thoughts, conversations, and work you have done so far in mind, design your invitations! Return to the "Opportunities Overview Worksheet." What method of invitation best fits in your church with these potential teachers? You see by now that the invitations issued this year are a step in a larger building process. Keep the largest vision and plan in mind at each step of the process, especially in making these key decisions:

■ Decide how you will make the initial contact with these leaders/teachers. Will it be done by phone or email, in a handwritten or preprinted invitation?

■ Decide how you will follow up that initial contact. Will it be by phone, email, or personal visit? Will you make individual contact or have a group event?

■ Decide who will make the contact. If you are working with a group of people, divide the names using your networking skills. Is there someone on the list whom one of the inviters knows well? (Note that some of us are better at inviting than others.)

You are ready to use the "Details, Details" and "Promises, Promises" worksheets (see appendixes D and F). Consider creating your invitation based on the information from these worksheets, perhaps in an intentionally selected font on paper chosen for the purpose with engaging graphics.

Depending on the mode of invitation you choose, you will also need to consider a concrete vehicle to give potential teachers the reasons you want them to become involved in the educational program and to provide them with the promises of support they will have when they accept.

When the decisions are made, use the "Opportunities Overview Worksheet" to create a master chart of the names of potential leaders/teachers, the kind of contacts to be made, and who will be making each contact. If you are giving some invitees a choice of where to serve, you may need to make a list of which contacts need to be made prior to other contacts, and create a system for ensuring your contacts are made in an orderly fashion. Select someone to keep the full list, making note of those who have accepted or declined as the people extending the invitations obtain this information. Set a date for checking back in with one another to review who has accepted and where there are still openings to be filled. Consider the sidebar examples as possibilities (see page 18).

10. Welcome the new teacher(s). Once a potential teacher has accepted an invitation to teach, you might think the work of inviting is complete—but it's not quite! It is important to thank the teacher for accepting the invitation to join in this faith-sharing adventure. It is also important to remind the teacher of the important events and dates that will begin his or her journey as a teacher in the educational program. *This step is the transition between the invitation to teach and resourcing the teacher.* Here are a few suggestions.

■ Attractively designed postcard with a thank-you note and upcoming dates on it

■ Greeting card offering congratulations or thanks with a handwritten note inside

■ Inspirational message or teacher-student cartoon in an email or Facebook post

■ Small gift, such as flowers, balloons, baked goods, or notepad with a thank-you message attached.

Intentionality Makes a Difference

After reading the preceding ten steps, you might be wondering if all of these steps just to invite teachers are really necessary. "We've been doing without all this rigmarole for decades, and things have gone just fine." Consider this old adage: "If you always do what you've always done, you'll always get what you've always got[ten]." You can probably get warm bodies in rooms by grabbing people in the hall and pressuring or guilting them into teaching Sunday school. However, with the life-transforming Good News of Jesus at stake, is that really what you want?

We encourage you to try these steps that increase your intentionality in identifying, inviting, and supporting teachers in the enlivening work of teaching the Good News in your congregation. With the best news ever as your message, the best possible fit of the teacher for each unique group of learners increases the likelihood of the transformation you hope for to start taking place. The invitation matters—may God bless your intentionality as you invite!

CHAPTER THREE

Equipping the Teacher

Denise Janssen

> Educating yourself does not mean that you were stupid in the first place; it means that you are intelligent enough to know that there is plenty left to learn.
> —Melanie Joy

Saying yes to the invitation to teach is the beginning of an excellent adventure, a fascinating journey! You made promises of support during the invitation process, and it's time to consider how best to go about providing teachers with the resources and support you promised. Truly effective teachers are constantly growing and learning, and ongoing education, support, and provision of tools helps.

A plethora of terrific resources exists to help teachers in the church to reflect on teaching. This chapter will provide a list of recommendations, but the reality is that many of those resources will not make it into the hands of the individual teachers who could benefit most from them. Perhaps some teachers read some of the latest scholarship on education, but the benefit of their learning stays largely within their own work.

Further, teachers in the church often do their work in isolation or in tandem with only a co-teacher or a Christian education staff person. Yet most teachers recognize the benefit of seeing their work as part of a larger team effort. Sharing ideas with others spurs creativity. Hearing how another teacher handled a difficult situation invites reflection and offers new perspective. Accountability to the group in teaching excellence helps everyone push through complacency and habit to integrity and transformation.

One of the most effective ways to address this issue is with monthly or quarterly gatherings—you might call this something like in-service training or toolbox time for teachers. The more investment teachers have in these gatherings, the more likely they are to find them valuable. Even if one person (staff, Christian education board chair, pastor) takes primary responsibility for continuing education, teachers can be tapped to share leadership in rotation, or they can bring brief critical incidents from their teaching for the group to think through and brainstorm about together. Encourage teachers to sign up for their turn in presenting ideas they have been unearthing through personal study or experience about teaching and learning in the church context.

Hopefully, adding or expanding teacher gatherings will be met with enthusiasm. After all, when we are talking about sharing the gospel in more transformative ways, surely those committed to the vital work of teaching and learning will be willing to invest a small amount of time in expanding their understanding and honing their skills. That makes good sense. Move forward with the initial assumption that those involved in teaching and learning in your congregation would, of course, want to participate. Start by inviting everyone and celebrating whoever decides to invest by attending.

Yes, such gatherings do take additional time. It is possible that, rather than celebrating their enthusiasm, you may find yourself navigating the concerns of those for whom investing additional time seems like an undue burden. Perhaps offer the sessions over a light meal at a time when people are likely together anyway, such as after Sunday worship or before a quarterly church fellowship event. Or maybe meeting at someone's home to share a potluck meal is more appealing. Offer childcare if possible. You know the preferences and needs of your group best. Be creative about what timing, location, and peripherals will "sweeten the deal" and entice more teachers to participate.

Many congregations have never expected anything more from teachers than to show up—hopefully prepared—and teach. If your church has "never done anything like this before" or if teaching training hasn't happened regularly, then creating a culture of ongoing learning, collegiality, and accountability among current and prospective teachers may well take some time. Apologizing for appropriately high expectations is counterproductive. Rather, set the bar unapologetically high, and it is far more likely to become the norm.

One more thing: also invite to training events people who aren't presently teaching but have an interest in learning more and people in whom you've discerned gifts for teaching. In this way, you create a new culture for those who may someday choose to teach. Over time, you may be able to cycle into the teaching ranks those who are willing to invest in learning and growing, which will ultimately transform the culture of the congregation from something like "doing enough to get by" to something more like "continually growing in faith, in skills, and in integrity for the purpose of transforming our congregation."

Ongoing growth and learning is crucial for teachers who seek to teach for transformation, not just information. If teachers are not learning and growing themselves, they will model for and communicate to participants that learning and growing are not really important. Even nonreligious disciplines recognize the need for ongoing learning. Physicians, architects, accountants, auto mechanics, and certified teachers in the public school system among others are required to participate in ongoing continuing education in their fields. Teachers in the church should too! And, more than other fields, the inner lives of teachers in the church matter and impact their teaching.

Noted educator and author Parker Palmer puts it this way: "Good teaching cannot be reduced to technique; good teaching comes from the identity and integrity of the teacher."[1] Many implications emerge from what Palmer is saying here. As teachers in the church, we cannot teach what we do not know. If we teach about grace in an ungraceful fashion, we unteach with our actions what we have tried to teach with our words. We cannot with integrity encourage students to an active prayer life if we do not pray.

I am not saying that in order to teach, a teacher needs to have perfected his or her prayer life, for who among us could ever teach if that were the case? Rather, it means that teachers need to develop an honest and genuine self-knowledge that enables them to reflect with participants about the issues and subjects they teach in a way that takes into account their personal experience. Ongoing growth in faith practices and life-long learning in matters related to faith are important components that help a good teacher become a great teacher.

Teaching the Teachers

Every year hundreds of new resources are produced and marketed to churches and individuals to help equip teachers. The sheer vastness of the offerings can be overwhelming, and it can be difficult to know what to choose and where to start in planning in-service gatherings for teachers in the church. What follows is a collection of books relating to teaching that make great in-service thought starters. Each of the books chosen could be the basis for a toolbox training, and each one is a resource I consider recommended reading. Pick one from this list and get started!

Baker, Dori Grinenko, and Joyce Ann Mercer
Lives to Offer: Accompanying Youth on Their Vocational Quests
(Cleveland: Pilgrim, 2007).

> Although the title identifies this as a book focused on youth ministry, many of the concepts and ideas in it are useful in ministry with children and adults, as well. We may think our ministry of Christian education is about ideas and concepts, but it is just as much about people and their life experiences. Companioning youth on their faith journeys—an idea from this book—is something we as teachers do at whatever level as participants bring their

questions and experiences to the learning environment. And participants at any age wonder about their unique gifts, about what God wants *them* to do. Discerning in community is a useful faith practice and could easily become the material for a lifelong learning event.

Bracke, John, and Karen Tye
Teaching the Bible in the Church (St. Louis: Chalice, 2003).

This is a small but powerfully practical volume focused on teaching the Bible, something we do all the time. Bracke and Tye, both professors and practitioners, consider the issues around teaching the Bible in the church through the lenses of how we learn, how we teach, and how we interpret and approach the Bible. This would make an excellent three- or four-part teaching training series but could also be used to create stand-alone sessions. The book is also readily understandable to laypeople while challenging laity and clergy to think more deeply.

Bruce, Barbara
7 Ways of Teaching the Bible to Adults: Using Our Multiple Intelligences to Build Faith (Nashville: Abingdon, 2000); and
Bruce, Barbara
7 Ways of Teaching the Bible to Children
(Nashville: Abingdon, 1996).

Buy these two books for your church library (or for each teacher)! Through the very helpful lens of multiple intelligences, these two books illustrate and explain the reality that each teacher and learner has different intelligences and access/assimilate information differently. The best parts of each book are the examples and ideas for incorporating greater variety in teaching adults or children using activities that better meet the differing needs of learners. Either or both could be used to create a fun, hands-on teacher training event.

Ferguson, Nancy
Christian Educators' Guide to Evaluating and Developing Curriculum (Valley Forge, Pa.: Judson, 2008).

> Ferguson's book will be most useful for the pastors, Christian education staff, and the board or ministry of Christian education as together they reflect on the aims and goals of the Christian education program in a local congregation. While the book focuses on curriculum (printed resources), the process and ideas could be developed into a retreat format or used as a guide in long-range planning for the congregation's educational program.

Galindo, Israel
How to Be the Best Christian Study Group Leader Ever in the Whole History of the Universe (Valley Forge, Pa.: Judson, 2006); and
Galindo, Israel
The Craft of Christian Teaching: Essentials for Becoming a Very Good Teacher (Valley Forge, Pa.: Judson, 1998).

> Galindo, in the comprehensive volume *The Craft of Christian Teaching*, gathers the best practices and foundational thinking from experts in the field of Christian education and distills them into brief and readable chapters. Chapters or groupings of chapters could be used effectively as the topics of ongoing educational gatherings for teachers. *How to Be the Best Christian Study Group Leader* would be a useful conversation starter as teachers dialogue about effective teaching practices (and what those practices teach by how they are employed).

Groome, Thomas
Will There Be Faith? A New Vision for Educating and Growing Disciples (New York: HarperOne, 2011).

> This book's title asks a critical question for those involved in the church's educational ministry (and beyond!)—will there be faith?

After all the teaching and the programs, after choosing the "right" curriculum and ensuring that the learning environment is optimal, the work of Christian education in the congregation boils down to this one question: will there be faith? Groome leads the reader in considering this important question through exposing a series of related issues and questions for consideration. In this case, choosing a leader or team of leaders who read the book and shape a teacher training event based on its insights might be preferable.

Harris, Maria
Fashion Me a People: Curriculum in the Church
(Louisville: Westminster John Knox, 1989).

In this groundbreaking book, Harris proposes that we take a broad view of education in the life of the congregation, positing that everything in the course of the church's life teaches. If we consider the whole educational experience of someone who participates in a congregation—not just the Sunday school classroom or Bible study—we can make formation in faith a part of everything a congregation does. Harris uses the helpful distinction between explicit curriculum—what we say we teach or the content of our printed resources—and implicit or null curriculum—what we teach by how we do things or by what we leave out. This work would be accessible reading for most teachers or could be distilled into a teaching training event with activities added to amplify learning.

Isham, Linda R.
Charting Our Course: Renewing the Church's Teaching Ministry
(Valley Forge, Pa.: Judson, 1997); and
Isham, Linda R., ed.
Embracing the Future: A Guide for Reshaping Your Church's Teaching Ministry (Valley Forge, Pa.: Judson, 1999).

Isham's work in these two books reflects the insightful and practical way in which she led ministries of Christian education at all levels, from congregation to region/conference to denomination. Both books are full of concrete ideas as well as thoughtful reflection, and either resource provides excellent material for teacher training, especially as new teachers take first steps in teaching.

Moore, Mary Elizabeth Mullino
Teaching from the Heart: Theology and Educational Method (Valley Forge, Pa.: Trinity Press International, 1998).

In this pivotal work, Moore puts several of the most effective educational theories and techniques in conversation with each other. This work goes beyond the nuts and bolts of Christian education to wrestle with theories about why we do what we do as teachers—without being too theoretical for lay readers. Plus, her writing style is enjoyable and engaging.

Palmer, Parker J.
The Courage to Teach: Exploring the Inner Landscape of a Teacher's Life (San Francisco: Wiley & Sons, 2007).

Palmer delves into the person of the teacher in this classic book written with educators of all ages and types in mind. Integrity, he argues, is key to authority in teaching. Congruence in what we teach and who we are or how we live is more important than being what we might think is a perfect role model. The whole book would make a great study, but chapters 1, 2, and 3 could each be used for stand-alone continuing education events or as a series.

Pipher, Mary
Another Country: Navigating the Emotional Terrain of Our Elders (New York: Riverhead, 2000).

This book is a must-read for younger adults who are teaching classes or ministering with older adults. While the book is not explicitly Christian in its context, the stories and ideas are immensely helpful for younger folks seeking to understand some of what it's like to be an older adult at various stages in the aging process. Reading this book can be an emotionally gripping experience. Pipher's book could also be used in a Sunday school class comprised of participants with aging parents seeking to understand their journey. The ideas/stories from the book could be paired with experiences common in older adulthood (simulating pain in walking, difficulty hearing, vision problems due to cataracts, etc.) for a practical and helpful teaching training session.

Roehlkepartain, Eugene C.
The Teaching Church: Moving Christian Education to Center Stage (Nashville: Abingdon, 1993).

This book by the late president of the Minneapolis-based Search Institute is centered on a unique understanding of education through the lens of a community's or individual's assets rather than deficits. Based on a major national research study, *Effective Christian Education: A National Study of Protestant Congregations*, the book offers insights and anecdotes regarding best practices based on this study from the late 1980s and early '90s. While the research is now a couple of decades old, the book's prescriptions for increasing the effectiveness of the church's educational ministry are still very useful, particularly for congregations who want to try something other than business as usual. This book would be useful as a platform for discussion among the board or ministry of Christian education, although teachers will also find helpful strategies and ideas.

Seymour, Jack, Margaret Ann Crain, and Joseph Crockett
Educating Christians: The Intersection of Meaning, Learning, and Vocation (Nashville: Abingdon, 1993).

This book, informed by solid scholarship, is profoundly concrete and practical while also being accessibly theoretical. The authors take a common human reality—the need to make meaning of life's experiences—and help readers see how faith at its essence is a meaning-making endeavor. The book is peppered with questions and exercises, making it useful for a group of teachers to read and discuss together, perhaps even sharing leadership. It could also be used as an individual study by teachers seeking to grow. Stories and examples are provided throughout. This book is sensitive to and useful in multicultural contexts.

Wimberly, Anne Streaty
Soul Stories: African American Christian Education
(Nashville: Abingdon, 2005).

Wimberly is a seasoned educator and expert in Christian education in the African American church. This book describes a process she calls "story linking" that connects our stories to stories of heroes and heroines of the faith, both in history and in Scripture. Hers is a powerful model that provides ideas and insights for teachers to incorporate into their teaching, in the African American church and beyond.

Yust, Karen Marie, and Eugene C. Roehlkepartain
Real Kids, Real Faith: Practices for Nurturing Children's Spiritual Lives
(San Francisco: Jossey-Bass, 2004).

Teachers will see children in fresh ways after being exposed to the ideas in this book. When we consider that children, too, have faith as a gift from God, we are challenged to help them grow in that faith—not just in knowledge of Bible stories. Yust and Roehlkepartain do a remarkable job of illuminating children's lives of faith and bringing parents and teachers together as partners in fostering their faith. Yust is a noted expert in child and adolescent spirituality, as well as a pastor and parent herself. You might consider purchasing copies for teachers of children and take turns leading sessions discussing the ideas from a chapter or two over lunch after church.

If the teaching corps of your congregation is in need of more basic how-to on continuing education, the American Baptist Home Mission Societies provides a series of workshops as free online downloads that may be accessed on their website at http://www.nationalministries.org/resources/church_life_leadership/index.cfm. These workshop teaching plans come complete with engaging content, recommended additional reading, handouts, and step-by-step directions for teaching the workshop.

Many other good resources are available that can provide the basis for enlivening teacher training experiences. Check the printed resources you may be providing for your teachers' use—these materials often offer suggestions for teacher training. Invite faculty in Christian education at a local seminary or church-related college to make a presentation. Denominational staff or Christian educators serving full-time in this capacity in a nearby congregation may also be good resources. You'll find a handout in appendix J titled "More Good Ideas for Equipping Teachers," too. With many options available, the question is not whether it is a good idea to be equipping teachers with new tools and ideas to enhance their teaching—the question really should be where should we start, and how soon can we get started?

Note

1. Parker J. Palmer, *The Courage to Teach: Exploring the Inner Landscape of a Teacher's Life* (San Francisco: Wiley & Sons, 2007), 10.

CHAPTER FOUR

What Do You Mean "Everything Teaches"?

Denise Janssen

> Nothing that is worth knowing can be taught.
> —Oscar Wilde

The above quote from Oscar Wilde reflects a truth about teaching, whether in the church or anywhere else, for that matter. Ultimately we cannot *teach* anyone anything. We can tell and demonstrate and illustrate and point someone in the right direction, but in the end, the task of learning is up to the learner.

This leads us to another truth about teaching: teachers do not determine the scope and sequence of what is learned, the "course" of the learning, if you will. Students determine what they will learn, as well as the depth and breadth of that learning. These two truths have powerful implications for the church's life and its educational efforts.

We might naïvely think that the only thing we're teaching in our Sunday schools is the material in the lessons. This is what educators call the *explicit curriculum*. But the truth is we are teaching far more than that. Our Sunday schools teach things *implicitly* by how things are done, and they teach things by what or who they leave out: the *null curriculum*. Sometimes students learn more of the implicit and null curriculum than they learn of the explicit curriculum. That's because learning happens better when there is an emotional connection—good or bad.

When we don't pay attention to the things that are taught implicitly or because they are left out, we may end up teaching things we don't mean—things that are inconsistent with the gospel we are teaching explicitly in our lessons. A good teacher can be cut off at the knees by things that don't need to become barriers to learning, and that same teacher can be supported in crucial ways by paying attention to the implicit and null curriculum. I like to think the five Ws and a bonus H that follow elucidate this idea.

Teach Who?—"Who" Teaches

Perhaps a more important question for the church than "Who should teach?" is the question of who should learn. For example, congregations make important choices when they decide who it is that has something to learn. If most grown-ups don't go to Sunday school or Bible study, that very fact teaches children, youth, and other adults something about how important learning is in the church and who needs to learn. When adults of all ages are learners, too, children and youth learn that growing in faith is a lifelong process.

Similarly, congregations teach something important by "who" among them teaches and at what age levels. Is the youth class always taught by a young adult because he or she can "relate," or do older adults have something to offer youth? Are teachers of children only women? Are they always the parents of the children in the class (which might give the impression to both the children and their parents that no one else cares)? Will any warm body do? Does the pastor ever teach the children or youth classes (are they important enough to warrant the pastor's attention)? Are schoolteachers the first people tapped to teach Sunday school, or is it understood that teaching science and teaching Sunday school may require different skills and gifts?

Myths abound regarding who makes a good teacher and who does not:

- "The youth want a hip young person who knows their culture and can relate to them to teach their class."
- "I can't teach the children's Sunday school class because I'm not 'good with children.'"
- "I'm too intimidated to teach a class of my peers. I'm not seminary-trained; I'm sure others know more about faith than I do."

For each of these myths, there are reasons that can be traced and understood as to why a potential teacher might feel this way. But usually these statements are unfounded.

Being a good teacher typically has three components: (1) giftedness, (2) personal qualities, and (3) training/equipping for ministry in this area.

Giftedness

Giftedness is a two-sided component of being a good teacher. It is true that "teachers" are among those in the Bible's various lists of ministries in the church for which someone may have special gifts. Probably we have all experienced a teacher who seemed particularly well-suited for the task. A number of excellent spiritual gifts inventories can be offered to help people discern their spiritual gifts.[1]

But there is another side to the idea of giftedness with regard to teaching, and it's a practical observation. Almost everyone, on a fairly regular basis, teaches some other person to do something, be it parking a car or using email or praying. We teach our children; we teach our spouses and friends; we teach our parents. Teaching and learning are happening all the time, and all of us are doing both. Truly, we are all teachers. Some are better at different kinds of teaching than others, and some have certain education or special training, but we all teach all the time.

Personal Qualities

This component of a good teacher has to do with the ways in which some people are just more enjoyable to be around and interact with than others. Personal qualities a teacher might have that draw students to them and inspire them to learn might include traits such as humility, consistency, honesty, authenticity, patience, and genuine caring for and interest in other people. Good teachers are also good listeners; are nonjudgmental, grace-filled, and not anxious; and have a passion for the stories of the Christian faith and a sense that teaching/learning is important.

Qualities such as these are important in teachers regardless of the age group they are teaching, and they override characteristics like "hipness" for teaching youth, "being good with children" in teaching children, and "knowing enough" for teaching peers or adults. Learning happens best when an emotional connection is made between the teacher and the student and the content. In most cases, that old adage "They won't care how much you know until they know how much you care" is true—and good teachers genuinely do care about their students.

Ministry Training and Preparedness

Finally, teachers may have great raw material—gifts and personal qualities—but without ongoing education or training, they likely will not be the best teachers they could be. Ongoing equipping for ministry is essential, and it needs to be modeled at all levels in all areas of congregational life. When ongoing education is part of the ethos of the congregation, the ongoing equipping of teachers more naturally takes place on a regular basis. And well-equipped teachers are better teachers, whether the raw material is great or just so-so.

When continuing learning is a part of the life of the congregation at every level, everyone is in the habit of learning and growing all the time. The education team or board of Christian education can give leadership, model continuing education, and encourage the ethos of continual learning. The level and type of ongoing learning that will be useful for each person differs based on the person's interests and skills, life experiences, and job skills. For some a seminary course might be appropriate to their ability and interests, while for others a workshop in group dynamics or learning styles might better address their concerns and areas of curiosity.

Continuing learning as an ethos in the congregation means that no one begins a new area or type of service believing there is nothing more to be learned and no new skills to be gained for that area of service. Rather, people must individually recognize they are a work in progress and take responsibility for their own continued growth in partnership with others in the congregation. In short, education is never "finished."

Teach What? and Why?— "What" Teaches and "Why" Teaches

One of the first questions raised when considering what to teach and why is this: What is the goal of teaching anything about faith? Becoming clearer about the purpose of teaching anything helps us better consider what to teach. In some congregations, the goal of teaching is informational—people of faith need to know some things about their faith (Bible stories, faith practices) in order to grow in faith. While it is true that some information is important, this way of understanding our goal stops short. Just knowing something doesn't mean that it will impact the way a person lives or acts, for example.

Teaching for transformation takes into account that some information is important but that information or knowledge for its own sake isn't enough. When we teach for transformation, we go beyond just sharing information to inviting participants to consider and discern together how that information impacts our lives and choices. Teaching for transformation invites learners to bring their whole selves to the table and to reflect on the information in light of their own lives and experiences. And transformation necessarily involves change, whether large or small, in response to new understandings. Teaching for transformation doesn't ensure that transformation will take place; rather, it recognizes transformation as the goal of the teaching and learning process.

Congregations often struggle with what to teach. These are important questions, because the "what" that's taught (the explicit curriculum) and the "why" it's taught (the motivation or goal) matter. A number of excellent resources are available to help congregations consider the question of what to teach as the answer to that question grows out of an understanding of what the congregation values and what beliefs it shares. An excellent resource to help congregations sort through the "what" and "why" questions is *Christian Educators' Guide to Evaluating and Developing Curriculum* by Nancy Ferguson (Valley Forge, Pa.: Judson, 2008).

Lest we confuse curriculum with the printed resource used in teaching, which is what many congregations think of when asked what they teach, let's unpack what is meant by "curriculum" in a fuller way. Noted educator Maria Harris offers this broader definition: "Curriculum is more than materials and technique. . . . We are moving toward a creative vision that sees all facets of the church's life as the church curriculum, with curricular materials named simply 'resources.'"[2] Harris goes on to describe how each aspect of the church's life is formative—it teaches those who participate. Therefore, "the entire course of the church's life"[3] becomes an opportunity for teaching and learning. That goes far beyond the printed resources we choose. It even goes beyond the set of ideas we intend to teach, the explicit curriculum. The answer to the question of "what" we teach has expanded exponentially—truly we are teaching and learning all the time through everything we do (or don't do) in the course of congregational life. What we say we teach, that is, what we choose to teach explicitly by making it the topic of Sunday school or Bible study or a study group session, is only a small part of what we are teaching and learning all the time.

This means that the work of the education ministry or board of Christian education is undertaken in the context of the broader life of the church. Coordinating everything we teach in all the other areas of church life would be a huge task, but paying attention to what we are teaching throughout the course of the church's life is worth the effort. Cooperating with other ministries within the congregation to consider what we are teaching by how we do things and by what or whom we leave out is a useful endeavor for the education ministry or board of Christian education. Working with the pastor and the worship team to ensure that aspects of worship and educational opportunities dovetail is worth the effort. What we mean to teach can easily be "untaught" when we don't pay attention to consistency in our words and actions throughout the life of the congregation.

This may be a good time to raise the issue of the null curriculum and how what is left out teaches. A good example of what is left out is diversity in examples and illustrations used. It could be argued that a congregation comprised primarily of people of the same ethnicity need not be aware of diversity in the examples and illustrations used. I would counter by offering this reminder: if all that children or adults see in illustrations are people who look like them, it is easy to believe that all God's people look like them or think like them. This is a dangerous delusion under which too much of the Christian church has lived for far too long. Whatever the makeup of the congregation, paying attention to diversity with regard to race, ethnicity, language, immigration status, gender, sexual orientation, ability, and age is important. This is true of language, images used, and examples offered in teaching. What is taught by what is left out can be a dangerous and harmful teaching and very difficult to unteach.

Teach When?—"When" Teaches

Imagine a really great teacher leading the youth Sunday school class at 7:00 in the morning or a wonderful teacher of older adults teaching a class at 8:00 p.m. In these two situations, it may not matter how capable and gifted a teacher was assigned to either of these classes, because the timing would be defeating the possibility of learning taking place. Not only are teens known for not being early risers on the weekend, but research tells us that adolescents learn better toward the middle of the day. Similarly, science demonstrates that older bodies assist more in learning toward the beginning of the day—not to mention that many seniors avoid driving after dark. These may be extreme examples, but when we fail to pay attention to similar realities, we set up learning situations that are likely to be less than effective.

"When" matters in a lot of other ways too. Consider children whose parents are divorced and share custody through weekend visitation; scheduling learning opportunities only on Sunday mornings limits how often some of these children can attend. Why should Sunday morning be the only time when Christian education opportunities are offered for children? Consider, too, what it teaches families when Sunday school and worship take place at the same time. It's very convenient and perhaps better than nothing, but do we really want to teach that worship is an adult activity and Sunday school, or learning and growing in faith, is an activity for children? Further, it becomes a drain on teachers when they are consistently unable to participate in worship and Christian education offerings themselves. In short, "when" matters, so we do well to pay attention to the "when."

Teach Where?—"Where" Teaches

Take a moment to imagine that youth class again. Perhaps the meeting time has been moved to 7:00 in the evening, a much better time slot! But youth arrive at the church to find the group has been relegated to the mustiest classroom in the basement, furnished with the couches deemed too worn and ugly for even the church rummage sale. For some, the mold and mildew embedded in the furnishings triggers their asthma or allergies. Earlier that morning, the older adults arrived bright-eyed and eager to learn, only to face a daunting climb to their second-floor classroom. Those who were no longer able to navigate stairs were forced to turn around and go home.

Where Christian education takes place carries with it many implications. Safe, clean, fresh spaces appropriate to the age group are crucial for every class of learners. When the most comfortable and convenient classroom is assigned to one group, while other classes get a space that is cramped, inaccessible, or shabbily furnished, those decisions communicate something about how much each group is valued. We say we value our elders, but we don't consider their unique needs and challenges. We claim to love our youth, but we relegate them to the furthest corners of church life where we don't need to hear or see them. We make a big fuss over our children when the cherub choir sings, but then we corral them in closet-sized classrooms while the grown-ups worship.

Beyond the classroom space itself, many kinds of learning take place best in other settings. Consider the benefit of learning about God's creation while being outdoors in nature. Explore the options for taking individual classes on a local field trip. Is there a common space in the church that might allow children and youth to engage in more activity—together or taking turns?

These alternative locations may not be possible (or recommended) for Sunday school every week, but providing other settings for learning in other contexts when it is appropriate can be very helpful. Giving teachers appropriate settings that contribute to learning makes their work easier than when they are working in a setting that is not conducive to teaching. The bottom line is "where" matters and it can enhance or impede learning.

Teach How?—"How" Teaches

"How" has to do with equipping teachers and making them aware of the best strategies for learning. Think for a minute about how you were taught as a child or youth. When I was a child, we learned through memorization and repetition. The teacher told us the story, and we filled in the blanks on our handout with the "correct" answers. We memorized a verse from Scripture and received a star for repeating it back correctly. We learned songs that had little to do with the lesson for the day so that we could perform them in worship on a specific Sunday morning each quarter.

We are likely to teach as we were taught and expect a learning setting to work as it did when we were the age of the learners. But research in teaching and learning tells us that not everyone learns the same way—so how could we expect the best learning to take place for all participants if we are only teaching using one method or strategy? As we become more experienced as teachers, we are likely to teach using the methods or strategies we prefer as learners. Those strategies may work well for learners who learn like we do, but not so well for those who learn best in other ways.

In his research into the human intellect, psychologist and Harvard professor Howard Gardner identified various psychological and biological capacities or potentials, which he later termed "intelligences." This research became the foundation for Multiple Intelligences Theory (MI). Gardner posited that while every person has each intelligence, each individual has a particular constellation of dominant intelligences. Over time, Gardner identified nine intelligences: interpersonal, intrapersonal,[4] bodily/kinesthetic, spatial, linguistic, musical, logical/mathematical, naturalist, and existential intelligences.

Educators have embraced MI theory with a passion and popularized treatments that have largely forced it into the role of learning style theory. Gardner has consistently held that MI is *not* learning styles, but rather the intelligences are about specific content. For example, teaching the names of the books of the Bible using a song is not the same as nurturing musical intelligence. However, Gardner has identified two primary educational implications of the theory: *individuation* of content based on the teacher's understanding of a learner's intellectual profile and *pluralization*, which involves teaching important ideas in several different ways. Many educators still find in MI theory a useful rubric for rounding out their teaching strategies. See Appendix S for more on using the intelligences as a guide for expanding teaching practices.

Encouraging teachers to creatively employ as many strategies as possible can help learners make connections with the ideas presented, adapting the printed resource as necessary. A very helpful couple of books on this topic are *7 Ways of Teaching the Bible to Adults* and *7 Ways of Teaching the Bible to Children* by Barbara Bruce.[5] Both resources provide concrete explanations of what each intelligence means and suggest activities that reflect those intelligences.

Learners and teachers are diverse in more ways than in our dominant intelligences or in how we learn. Teaching "how" reminds us to ask the question about the various ways in which we are diverse. It also calls on teachers to ask about learners with various physical, emotional, and mental abilities, making sure that the learning setting is hospitable to all. This may mean making special accommodations for learners to participate, being flexible about classroom space, and providing assistance to teachers who may need it. Team teaching is not only a good idea in terms of classroom safety, but it can also bring balance and rich diversity to the classroom.

Indeed, teaching "how" reminds us of the importance of fostering safety in classrooms for people of all ages. It may be unpleasant to consider that a child or vulnerable adult might be harmed in the church, but it is a possibility for which we need to develop plans and policies to deter and prevent. Please refer to the information provided by your denomination or your church's liability insurance company and to chapter 6 and appendix I of this book for more information and sample policies.

This chapter began with a statement about how we cannot really teach anything, recognizing that learners are in control of their own learning to a great extent. While that is true, we as leaders in the church's educational ministry and beyond do have the power and responsibility to set a tone and create an environment. By paying attention to the context we shape—being intentional about implicit and null teaching as well as our explicit teaching—we foster an environment in which learners are more likely to learn what we intend for them to learn. A people of faith are fashioned and formed through everything they experience in the course of the church's life. Intentionality matters.

Notes

1. Inventories are available both online (e.g., www.umc.org/what-we-

believe/spiritual-gifts-online-assessment) and in print (e.g., *Discovering Your Spiritual Type* by Corinne Ware [Herndon, Va.: Alban, 1995], or *Spirit Gifts*, a group study by Patricia Brown [Nashville: Abingdon, 1996]). Another helpful website is equippedforeverygoodwork.wordpress.com, where you will find links to other inventories and resources created for congregations interested in exploring the area of spiritual gifts and helping members serve in areas of giftedness.

2. Maria Harris, *Fashion Me a People: Curriculum in the Church* (Louisville: Westminster John Knox, 1989), 17–18.

3. Ibid., 17.

4. Note that intrapersonal and interpersonal intelligences are not the same as extroverted or introverted, which refers to personality typing popularized by the Myers-Briggs Type Indicator.

5. Barbara Bruce, *7 Ways of Teaching the Bible to Adults: Using Our Multiple Intelligences to Build Faith* (Nashville: Abingdon, 2000). Also, Barbara Bruce, *7 Ways of Teaching the Bible to Children* (Nashville: Abingdon, 1996). Both books provide easy-to-understand descriptions of each of the intelligences, concrete examples of activities to appeal to learners with dominance in each intelligence, and sample lesson plans that incorporate activities appealing to several different intelligences.

CHAPTER FIVE

Nurturing the Teacher

Diane Janssen Hemmen

In ordinary life we hardly realize that we receive a great deal more than we give, and that it is only with gratitude that life becomes rich.

—Dietrich Bonhoeffer

Feeling gratitude and not expressing it is like wrapping a present and not giving it.

—William Arthur Ward

The deepest principle in human nature is the craving to be appreciated.

—William James

"Thank you" is one of the most important phrases in any language. Saying thank you does many things. It acknowledges the appreciation of the one offering thanks to the person being thanked. It recognizes a relationship between two parties. It emphasizes the importance of the task done and the gift given.

Giving thanks is an important part of worship in most faith traditions. We offer prayers of thanksgiving when we gather for worship and study. The Bible is full of prayers and stories of thanksgiving. Numerous examples can be found in the book of Psalms, such as the close of Psalm 30, "You have turned my mourning into dancing; you have taken off my sackcloth and clothed me with joy, so that my soul may praise you and not be silent. O LORD my God, I will give thanks to you forever" (Psalm 30:11-12). We remember the encounter Jesus had with the ten lepers in Luke 17 and the further blessing of the one who returned to praise God and thank Jesus (Luke 17:11-19). And we have Paul's words to the Philippians in chapter 1, verse 3: "I thank my God every time I remember you." These words from Scripture set the tone for us and can serve as guidelines for remembering to say thank you to those who labor with and for us in the ministries of the church. "Thank you" is a balm that soothes the bumps and wounds that can come with serving in the church and particularly with teaching.

The teacher plays a pivotal role within the learning environment, similar in responsibility to that of a parent in a family, a manager at a restaurant, or a COO of a corporation. Teachers often set the tone of the learning experience. Teachers determine, to some extent, the scope of learning in a given session by the choices they make in planning based on their knowledge and experience of class participants. Teachers honor class participants by learning and using their names. Teachers

"Thank you" is just two little words, but they can mean a lot . . .

Thank you for opening the door for me.

Thank you for filling my water glass.

Thank you for listening to the story of my adventures in purchasing a car.

Thank you for helping my child through this tough transition.

Thank you for being the best mother a daughter could ever have.

Thank you for writing this book, which helped me understand quantum theory.

Thank you for teaching in our educational program.

can be a light of grace to individual church members in ways that are unique because of the opportunities for sharing created in small groups. Teachers go above and beyond the level of interaction most participants expect. Teachers look out for the well-being of participants in the vulnerable moments learning can create.

We all know that teaching is work: preparing, studying, creating a conducive learning environment, considering the physical and emotional comfort of participants, accommodating special needs, showing compassion when someone is having a bad day, and so much more. There is also deep joy to be found in serving God and others through teaching, and to that end, we want to help teachers magnify the joys and share them, while also supporting teachers as best we can with the more difficult aspects of teaching. As part of an overall culture of learning within a congregation, the care and nurture of teachers cannot be underestimated.

We nurture teachers in our educational programs in ways that are private and behind-the-scenes, as well as in ways that are more public and visible.

Nurture behind the Scenes

It is important to acknowledge that most teachers in the church are not seeking public accolades or thanks. In most cases, having a Christian education staff or committee that pays attention to healthy communication and follow-through makes the experience of teaching far more rewarding than public praise or thanks. We have an important first opportunity to nurture healthy relationships during the recruiting process. Being clear about expectations during the recruiting process sets the stage for the work that is to follow. In fact, clear and open communication about expectations is actually one way we honor and thank teachers. It is disrespectful, among other things, to conceal some of the details or expectations when we invite people to teach in order to get them to accept. If the invitation to teach comes without sufficient detail, or if the invitation not-so-accidentally "overlooks" some of the expectations of the role and work, naturally those accepting that invitation will feel resentment and distrust. If teachers have a clear understanding of the work that lies ahead and are not surprised by what is expected of them, they are less likely to regret responding affirmatively to the invitation to teach, and they are more likely to want to continue teaching or to say yes again in the future.

Some of the best ways to build acts of nurture into Christian education come prior to anyone actually teaching. We respect and thank teachers by recognizing that being a good teacher and doing a good job is important to most who agree to teach. For example, offer an orientation session or teacher training event well in advance of teachers actually undertaking their responsibilities. Such training not only nurtures teachers but also recognizes the importance of the work they are doing. Providing tools like printed resources and a well-stocked learning environment honors teachers and helps to allay the natural nervousness or fear of undertaking a new work. Nurturing gifts and healthy, life-giving practices through ongoing training works like oxygen for teachers who understand their role as part of their giftedness and vocation—and isn't that all teachers in the church, at least ideally? Chapter 3, "Equipping the Teacher," is full of great ideas for ongoing continuing education and training.

In the church, where budgets are usually stretched and staff are overloaded with responsibilities, demonstrations of gratitude and nurture can seem like just one more thing for which there isn't money or time. Keep in mind that nurturing teachers extends to simple things that don't cost money, things like honoring their time and resources. Demonstrating the use of tools—everything from the photocopier to the coffeemaker to a Bible dictionary to the thermostat—so teachers feel confident using them can be an act of nurture. And being available or having another volunteer to help troubleshoot problems that may arise can be a gift to a teacher who is trying to serve with excellence in the midst of a busy life. Nurture can also mean providing an updated list of specialty supplies available for use and ensuring that the teaching space is stocked with standard supplies and furnished as promised. If teachers have to spend time rearranging the classroom or run all over town searching for supplies, only to find them in the supply closet unbeknownst, they may well feel frustrated and unappreciated. And training teachers in the features of the printed curriculum, along with any supplemental resources to which they have access, further honors their time and takes seriously their gifts.

If teaching were only a matter of honing one's craft and efficiency, these strategies for nurturing teachers might be enough. But the most important teaching resources are the teachers themselves. I repeat Parker Palmer's words: "Good teaching cannot be reduced to technique; good teaching comes from the identity and integrity of the teacher."[1] He goes on to talk about the importance of congruence in the inner life of a teacher. Teachers who are doing what they teach are our goal. Nurturing our spiritual lives is critical if we are to teach others about spiritual things. Teachers minister to participants, and they, in turn, need someone with the internal emotional capacity to minister to them, as well.

Ongoing spiritual formation events and resources become an investment in healthier and more effective teachers. Continuing education provides opportunities for reflection on the work of teaching and how it impacts both the teacher and participants. In some ways, the best investment a congregation can make in the effectiveness of its educational ministries is in the spiritual nurture of teachers. Teachers need to be fed and to know that they are not alone in their task. Nearly every congregation has members who are unable to undertake other tasks because they are physically frail or shut-in, but these members could be invited to pray for teachers and to share a note each month or quarter, reminding teachers that they are appreciated and upheld.

Covenanting Together: Blessing or Commissioning Teachers

Acknowledging and ritualizing teachers' roles and their upcoming service to the congregation is critical. This type of support can have both public and private dimensions. Written words of thanks from those who have done the inviting as well as some public recognition suited to the given context seldom go without effect. Perhaps your congregation has a "Rally Day" or some sort of intergenerational event at the start of the program year or when children head back to school in the fall. Name and publicly thank those who have agreed to serve as teachers. Take a moment in the worship service to share a litany of commitment or other worship act with words of thanks and promises of support and prayer. Perhaps the church newsletter or bulletin could feature a listing of those who will be teaching along with a word of thanks from the officers of the church or from the pastor or another staff person.

Whatever approach is suited to your context, be sure to honor and to recognize teachers both directly and publicly. Of course, anytime names are read or printed, there is a danger of overlooking someone. Take care when recognizing people by name, but don't let the fear of inaccuracy keep you from naming and honoring teachers publicly. Such an event reminds the congregation of the covenant role teachers play in the life of the congregation, as well as reminding teachers when they are preparing and teaching that they are ambassadors on behalf of the congregation.

Offering recognition is also an important way to perpetuate a culture of invitation within a given setting. Not everyone will be able to teach every time he or she is asked. As you recognize those who have been able to say yes, be sure to offer other ways to be involved in the church's educational ministry—many of which will directly support the work of the teachers. If someone cannot serve this year as a teacher, maybe he or she will feel called to do so another time. And perhaps, in consideration of future service, the person who cannot teach this year will par-

A Vast Supporting Cast

The Christian education ministry of the church benefits greatly from having a vast supporting cast. Everyone in the congregation can be involved in this vital ministry in some way. Here's a creative way one couple found to support the educational ministry of their local church.

Elizabeth is a grandmother and matriarch of a congregation. In her retirement, she finds she is not as mobile as she once was, and she and her husband spend several weekends away visiting family and friends each quarter, enjoying their retirement fully. It is difficult for Elizabeth to agree to teach as she did for many years, but her commitment to the church's educational ministry remains high. She will do whatever she can still do to be supportive.

So one year at Vacation Bible School time, Elizabeth and her husband, Daddy B., found themselves drinking lots of Dr. Pepper, their preferred soda. A request for empty two-liter bottles and other craft supplies had gone out shortly after the VBS teachers were in place, and Elizabeth and Daddy B. wanted to donate as many empty bottles as they could. They knew that their son, daughter-in-law, and grandchildren would be participating in VBS, and they remembered fondly the significant learning times they had at VBS, both as participants and later as teachers. VBS was life-changing for them, and they wanted it to be so for their children and their grandchildren.

Finding some way they could support VBS, even if they couldn't teach or even attend, helped Elizabeth and Daddy B. feel a part of this important learning time, and it provided a useful resource for the program too.

Publicly recognizing, honoring, and nurturing teachers can have a widening impact in that it raises awareness of the church's educational ministry and creates a sense of investment that goes far beyond the teachers or Christian education committee.

ticipate in an ongoing teacher training event or invest in the church's education program in some other way.

Nurturing teachers extends to maintaining contact with the people who said, "No, thank you" to the invitation to teach but who may be willing to become involved in some other way, either occasionally or on a regular basis, to directly support a given class or the overall educational ministry. Consider having the individuals whose initial invitation was declined keep in touch with that person and renew the invitation next year. Or perhaps Christian education staff or committee members may accept responsibility for continued nurture of these potential future teachers. For some who couldn't say yes right now, the love of teaching may build slowly over time, leading eventually to an attitude like Elizabeth's that led her and Daddy B. to drink a little more soda than usual in order to do whatever they could to be supportive (see page 52). For the young adult or new member, providing some supplies for VBS one summer can lead to serving refreshments for a class next month, which may eventually lead to deeper relationships and deeper faith, and then finally to joining a teaching team someday in the future if that is his or her area of giftedness and Christian vocation.

"How May I Help You?" as an Act of Nurturing and Thanking Teachers

"How may I help you?" is another way of saying thank you and nurturing teachers. The simple act of asking this question lets teachers know they are appreciated and supported, that they are not doing this work all on their own. These are important words because they remind the teacher of the existing support system, a network or team ready to help when a need does arise. As a seasoned Christian educator with experience asking this question hundreds of times over many years, I can recall answers that ranged from "Could we have some Bibles?" to "All of our dry erase markers have disappeared" to "Don't need a thing, but thank you for asking." "How may I help you?" is a concrete way of expressing gratitude and valuing teachers' investment of themselves by ensuring that the necessary tools are provided.

That leads us to another way of nurturing and thereby thanking teachers: knowing teachers on a personal level is vitally important. Sorrows, celebrations, and significant life events affect the way we live our lives. Remember the Parker Palmer quote earlier in this chapter about teachers teaching who we are? Well, that's true when there are challenges as well as celebrations filling our lives. Being aware of teachers' life events enables us to offer a word of support and understanding. Sometimes it might mean finding a substitute teacher or gathering supplies or bringing the class snack. Sometimes it might mean offering a hug or a listening ear.

Consider for a moment how often your work colleagues have been impacted by something going on in your personal life or how often family members have felt the effects of events in your work life. Palmer's statement about teaching who we are is true far beyond teachers, extending to all the areas of our lives. Nurturing teachers is most effective when we know one another on a deeper level that enables us to know one another's needs and get to know how best to support and encourage one another. For small congregations that may feel at a disadvantage with regard to human and financial resources, this can be a place of real advantage where smaller numbers mean knowing each other better.

Particularly in smaller membership churches but true for churches of all sizes, nurturing teachers involves coordinating which requests will be made of which person. This is another place where knowing one another on deeper levels is helpful. Many small membership congregations (and some larger ones too) are blessed with a few people who do lots of things. If a person is asked to serve as a teacher this year, it is indeed an act of support and compassion to consider carefully before asking that individual to serve on the budget committee at the same time. It is especially helpful to have a committee in place to monitor the coordinating of responsibilities. In some congregations, this work is led by the pastor, perhaps working with a committee on nominations or leadership development. Multiple requests of the same person cannot always be helped, but paying attention to this detail is an important act of care and nurture.

"What Can We Do Better?"

An evaluative survey for feedback from teachers is yet another crucial way to nurture their growth. We all want to feel heard, especially as we become more experienced at doing something. No one will know better how the life of a class is going than its teacher and participants. Requesting feedback makes it possible to better equip and support teachers, and it deepens the relationships that are so important to the invitation and nurture process. Listening and asking for feedback is, in itself, an act of care and nurture.

The timing of an evaluative survey is critical for its productive use, both as a tool for investigating teachers' interest in continuing to serve and for allowing follow-up appropriate to any concerns that may be raised. A task force could be charged with just this project, or it could become the work of Christian education staff or a standing committee.

Another way to respect, honor, and nurture teachers is to be intentional in the creation of the survey to allow for honest feedback and critique. While a sample survey is included in appendix T, it is important to consider your own context, what you want to learn from the survey, your group's plans for upcoming program shifts, and other factors that may inform how you adapt a survey for your teachers. Those other factors may include creative ways of thinking about Christian education in light of culture shifts in a given community. A survey can do many things but ought not be expected to do too much. The format of the survey is also important, so consider carefully whether your teachers are more likely to respond to a paper survey or to something they receive via email or through an online service like Survey Monkey.

Myriad creative ideas for nurturing and supporting teachers are included in appendixes N and O. Refer to those lists to get started on your plans to nurture teachers. It is important to remember that not all good ideas will be good for all contexts or for all time. Think about adding/subtracting at least one thing annually as a way to stay engaged with the task of nurture and care for teachers as well as to provide that heightened sense of expectation to your gestures of gratitude and celebration.

Nurturing teachers, investing in helping them grow and continue to become the fabulously gifted humans God made them to be, is so important. Yet it is too often overlooked in favor of sharing new techniques or purchasing glitzy gadgets and teaching toys. Teaching demands a lot of energy—emotional, physical, creative, and spiritual. Finding ways to say thank you is among the very best means we have to nurture teachers.

Note

1. Parker J. Palmer, *The Courage to Teach: Exploring the Inner Landscape of a Teacher's Life* (San Francisco: Wiley & Sons, 2007), 10.

CHAPTER SIX

Coordinating the Congregation's Educational Ministries

Diane Janssen Hemmen

Alone we can do so little. Together we can do so much.
—Helen Keller

No one can whistle a symphony. It takes a whole orchestra to play it.
—Halford E. Luccock

If you are making your first turn out of the traffic circle here, with a chapter that considers how best to coordinate the work of your Christian education ministry, I'm glad you're here. Whether you are contemplating the formation of a committee or team charged with overseeing Christian education for your setting or considering ways to improve the effective functioning of a committee already in place, you've chosen a great beginning!

My grandmother often said, "Many hands make light work." How many times has someone used that phrase to remind us to continue our work or efforts at chores, or to join in and help others? Well, that little mantra applies just as well to our life together and to our work in the church. The more people with the same goals who are focused on a task, the more ideas for its success will be available! Experience suggests that when people come together to focus on a task as important as Christian education that their shared concern really does yield its own joy and fruit. When Jesus said, "I am the vine, you

Competing Roles

The Christian education ministry may find itself pulled in at least two directions: the group is both vision caster and detail chaser. Members of the ministry may prioritize detail-oriented tasks, such as making sure classrooms are appropriately supplied and printed resources are ordered on time. In the same moment, members of this ministry are called on to see the big picture and make decisions for the long-term health and well-being of the congregation's learning and growth. Team members may naturally gravitate toward one or the other—a helpful thing since the group's charge is likely quite broad. Some Christian education ministries find it helpful to create space and guidelines at meetings for doing long-range visioning; later in the meeting, they set aside time for reporting and organizing the details. Some may choose to do reporting in writing to be read outside of meeting time or to organize details via email or chat. Whatever your group's style, it is helpful to pay attention to the sometimes competing foci of the ministry's work so that they can be held in creative tension.

One more thing: how we name the group focused on the church's educational ministry is no trivial matter. What we call something goes a long way toward establishing what it is and what it does—toward defining its purpose and priorities. A "task force," for example, carries the connotation of short-term, episodic, and perhaps more detail-focused work. A "ministry" or a "team" gives the feel of permanence and visioning, or big-picture strategic planning. Many congregations need this group, whatever it is called, to do it all, but if your congregation has the option, consider how you name this group focused on educational ministry and what meaning is attached to what you call it.

are the branches" (John 15:5), the "you" was plural and communal, not individual. And the best of efforts in the church usually are only made better by the presence and shared concern of our brothers and sisters in faith.

A committee or ministry team may be a terrific way to approach the larger vision of Christian education in your context, because a committee can serve as the hub of this critical programmatic wheel, acting as nurturers and inviters and resource people. Together team members cast the vision, aligned with the church's mission. The team creates and proposes a budget, considering the big picture in the selection of printed curriculum and other resources. The team will take responsibility for inviting and nurturing, thanking and equipping, and making a case for the importance of education in all aspects of the church's life. They can keep the program in motion, taking up matters immediate and concrete, as well as matters more visionary and theoretical.

With all the things a Christian education committee or ministry *can* do, it is of primary importance to ask, "What *should* it do? How should it prioritize its work? And what shouldn't it do?" The answers to these questions depend, to a large degree, on what the church needs it to do—which may be determined by the size of congregation, its polity and history, and its healthy functioning.

Committees and ministry teams have a unique vantage point to consider Christian education with a broad view at important moments in the church's life. The committee holds in tension competing priorities and needs. Committees consider scope-and-sequence decisions, such as choosing between lectionary-based resources that follow the pastor's sermon and printed curriculum resources based on the International Lesson Series, which study a greater variety of biblical texts over a longer time period.[1] The committee is the group that makes sure the youth have a voice in choosing their teachers, that the small groups are well-resourced with handouts that follow the pastor's sermons, and that the older ladies' class has the resources and support to try some intergenerational activities with the young mothers.

Of course, a committee is only as good as its members. Gardeners can tell you that not all plants grow well next to one another. So, too, with a group of people; thus, we need to think about group dynamics as well as individual gifts when assembling a committee. Whether or not a committee is in place, it is wise to consider the different people who will comprise the group, what they bring to the table, and whether they will "grow well next to one another":

■ Do you need people with gifts in visioning and planning as well as details?

■ Do you need to include those people who themselves are currently teaching?

■ Do you need people who work well together, regardless of their particular experience with the church's educational ministry?

■ Do you need people with special skills or gifts to address needs in the church at this time in its life cycle?

■ Do you need people with diverse theologies and opinions?

■ Do you need to include people who are new to the congregation or to Christian faith, as well as those with more experience and history in the congregation or the faith?

■ Do you need people who have extensive connections to people either within or beyond the local congregation?

The length of time a person is asked to serve on a committee or ministry team needs to be considered beforehand and made clear at the time of invitation. Some denominations have a requirement about this in their *Book of Order* or *Book of Discipline*, and some congregations' bylaws specify terms served and provide a job description. These documents and guidelines should be consulted if they apply.

Just as it is helpful when inviting teachers to be honest with them about the various expectations that come with the position, it also is helpful and kind to be up front with committee or team members as much as possible. A committee, of course, will face certain challenges and changes that arise during the course of their service. They may even discern the need to change the conditions or term of service (to the extent permitted in your congregation's rules) based on their discernment of the congregation's needs or based on their vision casting. Regularly spending time together in prayer is important to the committee's work, as is at least an annual visioning or goal-setting time with time for building relationships and engaging in dialogue together.

When assembling the committee, take note as to whether members of the committee need to be grouped in classes, per your congregation's rules, so that several people cycle on or off of the committee each year, which provides for continuity. Because of the value of collective memory, a rotation of members each serving a given number of years but beginning and ending at different times can be a useful approach. If you're starting from scratch with a new committee or team, you may want to stagger the length of time each will serve (for example, two members for one-year terms, two for two-year terms, and two for three-year terms). In this way, you can maintain consistency and experience while ensuring new vision and fresh perspectives as some new members join the team each year. When inviting new members, you may want to consider who might be well-equipped to lead the committee in the future, who might be willing to take minutes or notes at the meetings, and so on. A sample calendar of the work of an education committee can be found in Appendix Q and highlights the many possibilities for pacing the work that may be assigned it.

The View from the Balcony

The work of the Christian education committee, at least in part, involves vision casting, strategic planning, goal setting, and prioritizing—and since curriculum involves everything in the course of the church's life, according to Maria Harris's philosophy (see chapter 4, page 39), the specific work of the Christian education ministry also needs to be coordinated with the larger vision and goals of the congregation. This work is kind of like going up into the balcony to get a broad overview from above. To get a sense of how different this view looks from a ground-floor view, it might be helpful to actually take the Christian education committee up to the church's balcony, if your church has one. If it doesn't, perhaps a second floor window will serve to illustrate the point. Peering down below, things look very different: some items appear in different proportion, different things stand out, and some things become unobservable from above. With this picture in mind, the committee is ready to begin its work.

Only very rarely does a committee get to begin working from scratch. In almost every case, a committee takes up work it inherits from previous members. It takes up a work already in progress with events already planned. A committee inherits a history complete with experiences (both good and not-so-good). Relationships among committee members likely existed prior to their work on this particular committee. Some have served before on this committee and remember "how we did that last time." Others are new to the work and ask, "Why can't we do it this way?" Rarely does a committee start fresh with a blank slate. This is both good and not as good. Mostly, it just is, and we need to recognize that.

The key roles of an education ministry team or committee are visioning, goal setting, strategizing, and prioritizing. Let's look at an example. Imagine your congregation is starting from scratch with a new Christian education committee. That new group would have to spend time in dreaming, dialoging, and praying together as they seek to lead the work of education in the congregation. The group would carefully consider what tasks to undertake immediately, deferring others as second and third priorities once the primary work is under way. Prioritizing is often the most complicated aspect of the committee's work, and it can be the most critical.

So let's imagine the committee has discerned the following priorities: congregation-wide small groups, a leadership training retreat, and children's after-school programming. Assembling small groups might be a primary strategy beginning in the spring, along with equipping the leaders and providing them with resources and training in their use. Significant work may be needed immediately with this strategy, but once the initial work is complete, those groups will continue to meet somewhat independently, with occasional needs for assistance and resources. Focusing on the small-group strategy first means the widest impact is felt immediately.

If it is already spring, the team may discern that it would be better to wait to start after-school programming for children in the fall when the children return to school. Adequate time for planning, staffing, and preparing the meeting spaces means longer lead times that help make for a better program. Perhaps the group decides, after an initial focus on the small groups, that they will plan a few Sunday afternoon events for neighborhood children and their families in the summer to set the stage for the fall after-school programming. By taking these two initiatives in sequence and thinking strategically, their workload is manageable and fun.

A longer-term strategy to be implemented may be a leadership training retreat. The team may decide to schedule it for the winter after the work of the nominating committee or leadership development team is completed and the next slate of church leaders are elected. While planning ahead for the leadership retreat, the education ministry team begins a series a mini-teaching moments at church council meetings. They set dates, secure leadership and a location, and begin promoting the leadership training event in the fall, once the children's after-school program for which they have been planning and preparing all summer is up and running. By strategically pacing themselves, the team is energized and not burned out. Evaluations from each new strategy help the team in their ongoing discernment and planning.

If that sounds like a best-case scenario, it probably is, but it isn't necessarily unrealistic. You may be thinking to yourself, *But our education team is overwhelmed with overseeing and supporting the Sunday school and a dozen other programs we've always done. There's no way this would work for our church.* There may be some truth to your ponderings. However, the "We've always done it that way" syndrome need not leave your congregation trapped in what has always been.

If the gospel we are sharing truly is transformational, and if our God offers grace and second chances, then perhaps we teach that message best by living it and letting go of what has always been just a little bit, enough to see where the glimmers of God's new work among us might be flickering to light. Set a goal each year of letting go of one activity or event "we've always done." Perhaps you'll replace it with a new initiative, or perhaps not; either way, you'll have a little more space for discerning the movement of the Spirit, who just might be leading in a new direction. Simply doing "what we've always done," with no room for fresh thinking and new strategies, can leave new team members feeling stifled and the group as a whole just going through the motions. Allow space for grace and new beginnings. If that's too difficult for a standing committee, then create a task force or working group to dream about and develop one particular new initiative.

More Reasons to Go "Up in the Balcony"

A Christian education committee has an important role in noticing things that may otherwise go unnoticed—things that make up the implicit and null curriculum as well as the explicit curriculum of our churches. For example, as discussed in chapter 4, the space in which a class meets is part of the act of teaching, and thus, the work of the Christian education committee must include attention to physical space. The Christian education committee is uniquely positioned to consider and to adapt for the better the parts of the education ministry from the broadest overview down to the minutest detail—from paint to glitter, from printed curriculum resources in each teacher's hand to one set shared by the group, from a rug on the floor to chairs that are appropriately sized to the students. By taking a broad overview of the whole program, a view from the balcony, the committee serves in this very important role of oversight and reflection.

The Christian education committee, with its unique view from the balcony, can observe and pay attention to important issues that might otherwise go unnoticed. Consider children whose parents are divorced and share custody: if Sunday school is the only formal education time then that significantly limits how often some of these children can attend and possibly with whom they can share the experience. The same issue becomes a limiting factor when parents who share custody must travel away from their church home to another city on weekends to spend time with their children. The committee can be tasked with considerations as foundational as whether Sunday morning should be the only time when Christian education and related activities are offered.

Consider, too, what it teaches families when Sunday school and worship take place at the same time. It's very convenient and perhaps better than nothing, but do we really want to teach that worship is an adult activity and learning and growing in faith (that is, through Sunday school) is an activity for children? Further, it can also become a tangible drain on teachers when they are consistently unable to participate in worship and/or additional Christian education offerings themselves. At the same time, if families are only able or willing to give one hour a week, then perhaps it is the best use of that time to offer part of the worship experience as a share family time and offer Sunday school during part of the hour—perhaps moving toward additional educational times in the future. Even just a 20-minute extension of children's Sunday school, maybe during the church's hospitality time after worship, can help provide a better concentration of time for teaching/learning while parents are happily occupied with coffee and treats and adult conversations.

A committee also can think about other overarching issues such as demographic shifts in the congregation or community that impact the effectiveness of the educational ministry. For example, one committee found themselves asking these questions: Does the youth Sunday morning class seem bigger than it has ever been, perhaps even outgrowing their room? Why? Has there been some shift in population, or are the new teachers the class helped recruit bringing a fresh approach the group finds engaging? Will those teachers continue? How can we understand and perpetuate this environment of learning and fellowship?

The Christian education committee can give voice to the concerns of people in the congregation who can sometimes become invisible: people with special needs, whether those needs come with age and decreased mobility or arise from differing physical, emotional, or intellectual abilities. The needs of hearing or visually impaired individuals can find voice with the Christian education committee. From caring for the special concerns of people on the autism spectrum to providing help for those with ADHD, from serving the unique needs of people with Parkinson's or Alzheimer's disease to ministering to those with Down syndrome or cerebral palsy, the Christian education committee has a unique responsibility to look out for those in the congregation who are so often overlooked.

In large congregations, this may mean consulting with experts in developing specialized programming or creating special adaptations. In small congregations, it may mean equipping the congregation with knowledge and tools to be able to accommodate persons with unique needs. In either case, the view from the balcony provides the Christian education committee with a unique vision of the gifts and needs of the people of God in their care.

Other foundational issues can include everything from identifying extra people to fill roles that are not specifically teaching positions (see also chapter 2, "The Invitation to Teach") to how to extend intentional, additional invitations to families to be the primary educators of the Christian faith for their children. One congregation even asked their Christian education committee to try to help them celebrate milestones with members—the first time a child stayed through the whole worship service in the sanctuary, the first time an adult served as a mentor to a baptismal or confirmation candidate, the first time a newer family served as a welcoming family for a brand-new family, the retirement of a long-term teacher from the women's class, and so on.

Some aspects of a committee's work are exceptionally concrete, such as creation and implementation of Child and Youth Protection policies and procedures to protect vulnerable people such as young children (see appendix I). There are subtle nuances to the committee's work. They will be the timekeepers of the program, both in the chronological sense as well as in the *kairos* sense of God's timing. Committee members will seek to discern when to let an idea die so that something else can start anew, to discern when to bring in new people or to go to the shelves to find again that printed curriculum resource everyone seemed to love three years ago. Sometimes the committee discusses confidential and sensitive matters, such as the need to honor a person for long-time service to the church's educational ministry and yet gently remove that same volunteer who is no longer able to carry out the work. Part of the ongoing work of identifying needs in a context is making the difficult decision that the program would be better off moving in a direction that someone or even some group is unwilling to go. The view from the balcony is an important vantage point for the Christian education committee in so many ways.

To that end, the shared prayers of the committee are important. Ongoing prayers of teachers and other members of the congregation become a vital lifeline. Remaining open to the leading of God's Spirit, reveling in the potential for creative and compassionate learning moments, focusing on the shared and sustained need for Christian education for everyone—the Christian education committee undertakes what is arguably some of the most important and influential work in the course of the church's life. So share these words as benediction with one another: "Go forth, Christian education committee members, and transform the world in partnership with our Creator!"

Note

1. Lectionary-based curriculum refers to print resources that use as their scope and sequence the Revised Common Lectionary, which is developed in a three-year cycle for mainline Protestant denominations

by the Consultation on Common Texts of the National Council of Churches. The International Lesson Series is a seven-year cycle of themes/texts developed by the Christian Education Committee of the National Council of Churches and becomes the scope and sequence for much of the children's and adult curriculum produced by and for mainline Protestant denominations. *Adult Bible Journeys*, produced by Judson Press, is an example of an ILS-based curriculum. *Seasons of the Spirit*, produced by Wood Lake Books, is an example of a curriculum that follows the RCL scope and sequence. Other curricula base scope and sequence on topics, themes, or books of the Bible, such as a ten-week study of the Gospel of John, or the popular Nooma video series. Scope and sequence refers to the breadth of material covered by the study and the order in which lessons are taught.

Conclusion

Sallie Verner

Don't let the pigeon drive the bus!
—Bus driver in Mo Willems's book by the same title

One of my favorite children's books is *Don't Let the Pigeon Drive the Bus* by Mo Willems. As the bus driver exits his vehicle, he tells the reader, "Don't let the pigeon drive the bus!" This gives the responsibility of decision making, of leadership, to the reader. The pigeon is very persuasive, using every argument he can think of to get the reader to let him drive the bus. The reader maintains his or her role as a responsible leader throughout the story.

If you are reading this conclusion, it is likely that you play a leadership role in your church's educational program, whether as teacher, Christian education committee member, staff, or pastor, or in some other capacity. These are not easy roles. There are many times when it would be easier just to let the pigeon drive the bus than to do the work we are called to do as we invite, support, and nurture teachers, or as we ourselves teach.

Somewhere inside you, you must "long for the endless immensity of the sea." You must dream of learners whose faith is transformed, of teachers and learners who share significant relationships, of growth and understanding that will move us toward God's new creation.

We believe the work of inviting, resourcing, and nurturing teachers is the foundation on which the educational program is built. You are doing significant work!

One last story: In *Traveling Mercies*, author Anne Lamott tells the story of a seven-year-old girl who got lost and was very frightened. A police officer who came to her rescue drove her through neighborhoods until she spotted her church. As she pointed to her church, she told the officer that he could let her out because she could always find her way home from there.[1]

As someone who teaches, or who invites, equips, and nurtures teachers in your church's educational program, you are giving a gift of grounding—the tools to find the way home—to teachers and learners in your congregation. The tools are the stories, poems, words, images, and relationships on which we build our faith and lives. You play a significant role in forming and strengthening those tools. Thanks be to God for you and for your work!

Note

1. Anne Lamott, *Traveling Mercies: Some Thoughts on Faith* (New York: Pantheon, 1999), 55.

AFTERWORD

As I read the manuscript for this book, I found myself more and more excited. At last! A succinct resource for congregations that provides both a vision for intentional Christian education and the concrete suggestions that bring the vision to fruition. Few, if any, other resources like this are available. Most are either theoretical without practical application or practical without the vision for ministry and formation. This one is both theoretical and practical.

Meanwhile, mainline Protestant congregations are struggling to find their way. Denominations are dwindling. The population of the United States is increasingly secular, and more and more people do not claim any religious affiliation at all. We cannot count on the general culture to nurture Christian faith. We should learn from our Jewish brothers and sisters who take seriously the imperative to form identity from birth to death. Like them, we must form Christian identity and show people the way to live their baptismal vocation. And too many congregations are doing a woefully bad job of it!

The authors of this book are clearly experienced in the challenges and possibilities for teaching and learning in congregations. In addition, they are comfortable with the best theoretical materials in the field. Denise Janssen and I have taught courses together, and I know that she is a gifted teacher. Her coauthors are evidently fine teachers too. It shows in every chapter. They have produced a wonderful little book. The chapters explain the what, why, and how of learning and growing in faith. The appendix provides twenty-plus lists and inventories that will aid in planning for effective education ministry.

Denise Janssen wrote in her preface that the work of religious education in Protestant churches is not so much about learning the answers.

It should be focused more on discerning the questions. This is an important clue to the approach to Christian formation taken by these authors. They understand that forming a vital faith is something that happens in an individual. It cannot really be *taught*, but it can be learned. And everything that happens in a congregation is potentially forming the faith that an individual learns. So, when congregational leaders begin to think more holistically about how to shape a congregational culture that allows people to discover their own questions and seek to learn in response to those questions, then vital faith begins to emerge in more and more children, youth, and adults.

Identifying the people with gifts to stimulate those questions and resources to address them is therefore one of the key tasks in any congregation. In my experience, congregations that skate over the inviting and equipping of teachers are headed for a slow death. A warm body in the room is not sufficient. We all need models who are deeply in love with God and whose gracious interactions teach us about the grace of God. Good teachers help us integrate the events of our lives that raise questions about the meaning of life and ultimate values, the questions that faith addresses. The authors of this book offer many suggestions and strategies for finding the right people to lead your educational ministries and how to supply resources so that they will be effective and joyous in their teaching ministry.

This book challenges congregations to "...teach in order to participate in the transformation of people into disciples of Jesus Christ, into bearers of the gospel in the world, and into agents of transformation themselves."[1] This is no small vision, but it is the only faithful vision. Forming disciples is the work of the whole church. This little book gamely shows us the way and challenges us to bigger thinking. Give it a try!

—Margaret Ann Crain
Professor Emeritus
Garrett-Evangelical Theological Seminary

[1] From the chapter "Why Teach?" by Denise Janssen.

APPENDIX A

Triage Worksheet

Check all that apply.

___ My congregation needs help identifying and inviting the right people to teach. (chap. 2)

___ I'm not sure how to tell if my congregation has identified the right people to teach at every level. (chap. 2)

___ Teachers in my congregation feel burned out. (chaps. 3, 4)

___ Teachers in my congregation need additional support and training for their work. (chap. 3)

___ Education is so important—how can we get people to see this and join in the work? (chaps. 1, 2)

___ My congregation has become so disorganized in our approach to education. How can we recast a vision for education for everyone? (chap. 6)

___ I'm the only staff person, and I need to get fifty-two teachers started next week! (chaps. 2, 4)

___ I didn't take the first course in education in seminary or with my lay training. Where do I start to evaluate the current education efforts of my congregation? (chaps. 3, 5)

Know Your Context Worksheet

This worksheet is designed to be especially useful to a committee or ministry team as they seek to understand their congregation and the different impressions each has of it. On a scale of 1–5, with 5 being highest, indicate how true each statement is for your church.

___ Our congregation is actively involved in transformational Christian education at all age levels.

___ Our congregation is committed to creative, enlivening Christian education for children and youth in the church.

___ Adult classes or small groups have strong group identities, don't vary in attendance much, and tend to meet together as a group for study over many years.

___ Education in the faith is more about knowing the details of the stories of our faith than it is about applying them in everyday life.

___ Formation in faith is the focus of our church's education program; thus, we focus a lot on applying ideas we are learning in everyday life.

___ Educational programs in our congregation involve many adults who are relatively new to faith and need a foundation in the Bible stories and spiritual disciplines.

___ The Christian education offerings at our church are appropriate to the level of education of the adults in the class.

____ Some adults in our congregation have literacy issues and struggle with reading.

____ People in our congregation tend to become more resistant to change as they grow older.

____ People in our congregation love to try new things and welcome meaningful change.

____ People in our congregation typically can't wait to retire so they have more time to volunteer to help others, grow, and study, etc.

____ Education in general, and critical study of the Bible and faith issues, is valued by many people in our church.

____ Our pastor welcomes the crucial role he/she plays in the church's educational ministry.

____ Our congregation has members at every stage of life, with people from across the spectrum of ages participating actively in educational ministries.

____ Our congregation is actively involved in hands-on mission and justice ministries in our community.

Now compare your answers to each question, Hear each other and listen seeking to understand the opinions of others. Discuss questions where there was a significant difference of opinion. Remember to listen charitably and conduct your dialogue with civility and grace.

Finally, identify which of these statements about your congregation are most important to you. Which ones matter most? What statements would you add to fill out the picture of your congregation? Try to include more assets than deficits. Knowing your context is an important first step to help you consider where your congregation needs to grow, as well as to assess vitality and health.

APPENDIX C

Teacher Qualities and Characteristics Worksheet

Complete this worksheet (if you are working with a team, each member should complete one on their own) using the scale 1 = most important, 2 = somewhat important, 3 = not very important. When working in teams discuss your results (respectfully) and try to come to some consensus about the most important qualities for teachers in your congregation.

A teacher in the Christian education program is someone who:

____ Is a member of this church for at least six months
____ Enjoys the age group he or she is asked to teach
____ Knows the stories of the Bible
____ Wants to learn the stories of the Bible
____ Understands the developmental characteristics of the age group he or she is invited to teach
____ Is enthusiastic about teaching from the printed resource or other curriculum provided by the church
____ Is willing to make a commitment of time, energy, and creativity to the educational program
____ Works well with others (a team player)
____ Is a good storyteller
____ Can be creative with crafts
____ Can lead singing
____ Has experience as a teacher
____ Has an outgoing personality or a welcoming presence

76

____ Makes people feel at ease
____ Can adapt curriculum/lessons to the learners and context
____ Can adapt to changing situations and thrive when circumstances change
____ Generally plans ahead or prepares well and follows through on responsibilities he or she accepts
____ Lives a life that evidences a steady, faithful transformation
____ Is willing to join learners where they are and help them take next steps
____ Understands teaching as a relationship

List any additional characteristics below:

_____

_____

_____

_____

_____

_____

_____

_____

Details, Details
Clarifying the Invitation to Teach

Working together, come to a set of expectations generally made of all teachers in your congregation. You may want to use this worksheet as the basis for a job description.

Teachers are invited to:

____ Teach (age group) the stories of our faith using (curriculum) and Bible

____ Teach from (dates, e.g., September 10 to May 31)

____ Work with a team of teachers/another teacher/alone

____ Be in the classroom from (time, e.g., 9:30 a.m.–10:30 a.m. or 5:00 p.m.–7:00 p.m.)

____ Spend a minimum of two hours a week in preparation

____ Be willing to attend at least one training/orientation event per quarter

____ Make contact with the each participant outside the class at least once each quarter

____ Engage participants from time to time for brainstorming future class topics

____ (Add your own.)

____ (Add your own.)

Standard Supplies Every Classroom Needs
(Plus a Bonus Wish List for Your Supply Closet)

1. Pencils and/or pens
2. White unruled paper (copy paper works)
3. Crayons and/or markers (washable are best for children, permanent for youth and adults)
4. Bibles (NRSV in youth and adult classrooms; easy-to-read paraphrase or story Bibles for children's classrooms)
5. Dry erase board with markers and eraser (alternately, chalkboard or newsprint)
6. Basic Bible resources (one-volume Bible dictionary and commentary—e.g., Harpers, Anchor; maps of the Middle East and Palestine during Bible times; concordance; world map or globe)
7. Wi-Fi—participants can access the Internet from their smartphones or tablets, which makes the basic resources and Bible available to everyone all the time (apps also work well)
8. Glue sticks (or glue)
9. Tape—masking and transparent tape
10. Paper clips
11. Stapler
12. Hole punch
13. Scissors (appropriately sized for the participants and teacher)
14. Chairs and tables (appropriately sized for participants, and in adequate numbers; children's classrooms may also want a story rug or carpet squares for storytime)

15. Waste bin and recycling bin

Some extra supplies that are really helpful to have in the classroom:
(Recommended: Stock a supply closet of less frequently used supplies.)
- TV/DVD player (also plays CDs)
- computer with Internet access, printer, and projector or classroom-sized monitor
- name tags (permanent or disposable)
- musical instruments and rhythm instruments
- napkins/cups for refreshments
- disposable or vinyl tablecloths
- LED candle, tablecloths in liturgical colors, and other symbols for worship center

Supply Closet Wish List Contents

aluminum foil
baskets
clear contact paper
cling wrap
construction paper
  (8" x 11")
cookie cutters
craft sticks
crepe streamers
dry erase markers
  (back-up replacements)
egg cartons
envelopes
fabric scraps
felt (for banners)
first aid kit
fishing line

glue gel
hangers
magazines with lots of pictures
magnet strips/rolls
name tags
notecards (3" x 5")
paintbrushes
paints: acrylic, tempera,
  watercolor, and finger
paint shirts
paper bags
paper fasteners
paper plates
steam iron
steam iron
stickers, stars and Christian-
  themed (Bibles, crosses, etc.)

play dough
Post-it notes
Q-tips
ribbon
rocks (small round ones)
rubber bands
safety pins
shells
sidewalk chalk (and/or pastels)
spools
spray sealant

sticky tack
string
tissue paper (colors/white)
toilet paper and paper towel
  rolls (empty)
toothpicks
wax and old candles or crayons
wax melter
yarn
zip-lock bags

Promises, Promises:
We've Got Your Back Worksheet

Teachers are promised:

____ Curriculum resources for every participant

____ Curriculum resources for every teacher

____ Physical space appropriate for the age group and number of participants and teachers

____ Standard supplies in the classroom

____ Supplemental Resources (media, books, games)

____ Equipment (CD or MP3 players, TV and DVD player, wifi, projector with computer)

____ Training (quarterly or monthly?) (group, individual, or online?)

____ Prayers for the teachers and participants

____ Help with problems/issues that arise—name who will generally be where

____ (Add your own)

Opportunities Overview Worksheet

Provided below is a model you can adapt as an Opportunities Overview Worksheet. You will want to format it to meet your congregation's unique needs.

Educational Program: Vacation Bible School

3- and 4-Year Olds: 2 teachers needed
1. Suzy Lovetoteach
2.
3.

Kindergarten: 4 teachers needed
1.
2.
3.
4.

Craft Specialists: 2 leaders
1. Gregory Glueandglitter
2. Angela Artsy-Craftsy

APPENDIX H

You Might Be a
Sunday School Teacher If . . .

A humorous list with truth sprinkled throughout! Select a handful (or add your own) to feature in a bulletin insert, teacher invitation, or other recruiting promotions.

You might be a Sunday school teacher if . . .

1. Security officers come to ask you why you have been cruising the aisles of the craft section at Michaels, Jo-Ann Fabrics, or Hobby Lobby all morning.

2. Your eyes tear up at baptisms/dedications of infants and children when the congregation promises to help the families raise their children in the faith.

3. You go early to church school because you recently saw a movie or read a book that you thought displayed intriguing images of God and you are hoping for a conversation with a like-minded person.

4. You buy a particular kind or size of product because you know the container could be used as a craft supply. You collect empty paper towel rolls next to the trash and recycling bins in your house. The church custodian saves things the church uses for you.

5. You read articles about how the brain of a five-year-old develops or watch PBS specials detailing the latest research on how adults learn.

6. When you walk into the room at coffee hour you notice the kids don't have a place to gather and you start thinking about how to fix it. Maybe you even find yourself having a picnic on the floor with them!

7. On several occasions you have found yourself in the children's sec-

tion of the bookstore when you went there to buy a new mystery novel.

8. You know where to find resources in the public library. The reference librarian knows you by name and pulls things for you that she or he thinks might be helpful.

9. You own an iPod or MP3 player and consult with youth at your church about what to download next.

10. You make connections between your work life and your spiritual life and enjoy sharing your thoughts with others.

11. People walk up to you at church to ask about a Scripture passage that troubles or thrills them. They know you'll understand.

12. You choose to sit in the section of the sanctuary where youth or college-aged people sit even though you have no one of that demographic sitting with you.

13. You read the announcements describing educational opportunities in your congregation and picture yourself participating.

SAMPLE Child and Youth Protection Policy and Procedures*

You will want to consult your judicatory office and church insurance company when creating your own set of policies and procedures, but every congregation needs to have policies like this.

Policies for Volunteer and Paid Staff Working with Children and Youth Church-Sponsored Events

Persons must be at least five years older than the age group with whom they are to work.

Two-adult rule: Two adults (not married to each other) must always be present in groups of children, except in emergency situations and where not reasonably feasible.

Ratios of adults to children (after two-adult minimum):
- one adult for every five preschool and elementary-age children
- one adult for every five to seven sixth- to eighth-grade children
- one adult for every six to eight ninth- to twelfth-grade children

When the two-adult rule is not feasible, an adult will be required to spot check or make unannounced visits as necessary. Doors are never to be locked and are to remain open.

---

*Adapted from the document mandated by the 1996 General Conference of the United Methodist Church, November 2009, for Gurley United Methodist Church.

Children must not be alone with only one adult without being visible to others in the immediate surroundings. If you find yourself alone with a child, the church's action plan is first to attempt to locate other adults in the area, and if unable to find anyone, move with the child to either the kitchen or nursery and then call for another adult to come to the church, beginning with the lead pastor. Maintain open doors and open blinds or windows at all times.

All staff and volunteers will be required to read and sign that they understand the guidelines for working with children and youth at church events. This will either happen at a training session or be completed on the church/denominational/judicatory website [website URL] and turned in to the lead pastor or youth pastor.

Transportation

A volunteer should not be alone with a child in a vehicle. If at all possible, find another adult to ride in the vehicle and call ahead to the child's parent or guardian. The church will maintain a file with medical permission form information to provide to a doctor in case of emergency.

- Everyone must wear seat belts
- No one weighing <85 pounds sits in the front seat

A driving record check will be done on the driver, in line with the church's auto insurance. If you have had more than six points in the past two years or fourteen points in the past seven years on your license for violations, you will not be able to transport children and youth.

If a charter bus is rented, ask the coach company if a background check is done on their drivers. If not, look for another charter bus company.

Overnight Trips

In public areas, make sure to keep an eye on the restrooms, which are an area of particular vulnerability.

■ Provide manageable ratios of adults to children that provide a fairly close gender equivalency to participants, with a minimum of two adults (one of each gender during coed activities).

    ■ one adult to every five elementary-age children

    ■ one adult to every five to seven sixth through eighth graders

    ■ one adult to every six to eight ninth through twelfth graders

■ Lodging arrangements:

    ■ Most youth areas have a cabin-style room with mobile bunk beds. In this setting, the adults should stay with the youth because of the numerous observers available in the room.

    ■ In a hotel-type setting or dormitory, "It is recommended that youth be assigned to rooms and adults be assigned to separate rooms. If possible, make the room assignments so that the adult room is in between two youth rooms. It is also recommended that the adults arrange among themselves to check on the youth rooms on a random schedule during the night. If you have a volunteer to take the night shift, that person can monitor comings and goings. If possible, choose a hotel where the rooms open to the interior of the building rather than the outside."†

Requirements for Becoming a Volunteer

■ We require all volunteers working with children and youth be members of the church for at least six months prior to an invitation to serve. Although church membership is strongly encouraged, other volunteers are welcome who fit at least one of the following criteria:

1. Fill out an application and provide reference information, including former church if they have not been attending the church for at least six months.

2. Are active in and regularly attend Sunday school and worship services.

3. Have a relationship with and obtain background clearance through the church.

4. Maintain membership in another church, provide a reference from their home pastor, and obtain background clearance through the church.

■ All volunteers must complete and return the volunteer information form.

■ Potential volunteers who have not been members for six months must complete the interview process conducted by the youth or children's staff or volunteer representatives.

Background Screening

References will be checked. A background screening will be provided for all in the church who work with, teach, counsel, or chaperone children at any church function. Applicants must sign the agreement authorizing the screening process approved by the church, and background screenings will be kept in the church's safe deposit box at its local bank, where access is limited to the current lead pastor and an appointed lay leader. The church is responsible for safety of this material and for the confidentiality of the report results.

■ Background screening results must come from the screening organization and not from the individual.

■ Background screenings will be repeated every three years, along with a Child and Youth Protection Policies training recertification.

■ If someone is not background screened and trained in Child and Youth Protection Policies, he or she will serve in an indirect contact function, such as serving food, under the supervision of a qualified church volunteer or staff member.

Reporting Suspected Abuse

State laws require voluntary reporting of child abuse in faith-based ministry settings. In keeping with Christian beliefs that children should not be abused and neglected, the church will practice and advocate immediate compliance with state laws suggesting reporting of suspected abuse/neglect of children and vulnerable adults whether or not it is required by law. Notification is requested to be made to one of the following: the lead pastor or youth pastor. A list of appropriate agencies and phone numbers follows at the end of this document.

Reporting Procedure
If you suspect or are privy to knowledge of abuse in the church setting or involving church members, do the following:
   1. Contact the lead pastor or youth pastor.
   2. Call the authorities.
   3. Fill out an abuse report (found in the library next to the mailboxes).

If they are not immediately available (within an hour), do *not* wait for the lead pastor or youth pastor to respond before calling the authorities. Fill out the abuse report while waiting for the authorities to arrive.

   ■ The lead pastor will remove the accused person from leadership and contact the supervising judicatory.

   ■ The lead pastor and supervising judicatory will notify the communications department of the judicatory/denomination.

   ■ The media response should be handled only by the appointed judicatory.

   ■ If the lead pastor is accused of abuse, the youth pastor can directly report the incident to the supervising judicatory.

If you suspect or are privy to knowledge of abuse outside the church setting, take these steps:
   1. Call the authorities.
   2. Fill out an abuse report while waiting for the authorities.
   3. Contact the lead pastor or youth pastor.

Since in this case the abuse happened outside the church, the lead pastor or youth pastor provides pastoral care and support for the victim and the person reporting and cooperates with authorities in their investigation.

Nothing in the accomplishment of this policy is intended to call on a pastor to violate the confidentiality of confession or clergy counseling relationship. Because of the complex nature of child abuse reporting, training and consultation will be available to clergy and laypersons to prepare them for a faithful response.

Response Procedures

A quick, compassionate, and unified response to any alleged incident of child abuse is expected. All allegations will be taken seriously, with grace, including privacy, shown to *all* parties. In view of the fact that people's lives can be greatly affected, only the lead pastor and youth pastor are to be notified. Church personnel are not to undertake an investigation of the incident. However, in all cases of reported or observed abuse in a children's or youth activity, all those present should be at the service of official investigative agencies.

Outside Groups Meeting in Your Church Facilities

The board of trustees (as the body responsible for the church's physical plant and use of its facilities), will require outside groups working with minors meeting on church property to review and agree to comply with the Child and Youth Protection Policies and Procedures as specified in this document.

This policy still holds true for organizations that perform their own background screening and train their own leadership, such as scouts. These organizations must submit a copy of the screening and training documents to the lead pastor. No documents that are more than three years old will be accepted and must be updated as specified for church volunteers. The documents must be reviewed and approved before the organization is allowed to use church facilities.

Agencies and Phone Numbers

Emergency Services 911
Police (nonemergency)
County Sheriff Department
Family and Children's Services
Rape Response Helpline

† Joy Thornburg Melton, *Safe Sanctuaries for Youth: Reducing the Risk of Abuse in Youth Ministries* (Nashville: Discipleship Resources, 2003), 94.

APPENDIX J

More Good Ideas for Equipping Teachers

1. Prepare and distribute materials to support the curriculum for liturgical seasons. For example, provide a handout describing the symbols of Lent, a matching game with pictures of the symbols for preschoolers, a bookmark with information about the history of Pentecost, a table tent with family mealtime prayers for Advent. Display examples of art, music, crafts, and other learning activities for liturgical seasons and specific Bible stories included in the curriculum.

2. Offer supplemental background information from commentaries or Bible dictionaries for upcoming Bible stories in the curriculum. Get a membership for your church at a local Christian Education Resource Center (various locations across the country) or sign up for borrowing privileges at the local seminary or Christian college library. Provide a resource library at the church (online would be even better) for teachers to use in preparing for their teaching.

3. Provide a link on the church website where teachers can connect to recommended websites for craft ideas, handouts and puzzles, informational articles, and articles with teaching tips, etc. The internet is an unedited collection of resources, and many teachers appreciate help navigating the best supplemental resources.

4. Provide periodic training on equipment: how to use the copier, the button maker, the laminator, other office machines, the TV/DVD player, projectors, etc. This training can even be made available to others interested in supporting teachers by troubleshooting equipment use for a teacher or group of teachers (who knows, you may

even be cultivating interest in teaching via technology with which they feel comfortable).

5. Set up a hands-on workshop-style enrichment series for teachers: how to match lessons with activities, how to lead songs, how to use multiple intelligences when planning lessons, how to create games as learning activities, how to do crafts, etc.

6. Provide lunch and learning opportunities: during a one-hour lunch time frame, provide a simple lunch and lessons. For example: how to incorporate audio/video resources into a lesson plan, biblical background on next week's Bible story, tips for working with children with specific issues, helps for facilitating a discussion, insights into the unique spiritual needs of youth as they develop their spiritual lives, the art of storytelling, etc.

7. Attend national or regional conferences together to get ideas and to get your batteries recharged. Wonderful education opportunities are sponsored by your denomination, region, or conference; local seminaries and colleges; parachurch organizations; etc. Attending together can create a synergy of new ideas and fresh energy.

10 Ways to Say Thank You

1. Send a postcard or email at an unexpected time.

2. Send a card for significant holidays when people might not receive cards, such as Thanksgiving or Valentine's Day.

3. Have a brunch before or after the church school hour to honor teachers and provide a time for them to visit with each other. Or offer good coffee and pastries early on Sundays.

4. Give teachers a homemade gift of food (a small loaf of bread or a jar of jam) with an attached note of thanks for their work. A framed photo of the class with the teacher makes a nice gift too.

5. Make a donation in honor of the teachers (e.g., sanctuary flowers at Easter or Christmas, resources for the library, children's books for the classrooms) with a note in the bulletin or newsletter about this gift.

6. List the names of the complete group of teachers in the bulletin and newsletter soon after they have accepted the invitation to teach, with encouragement for the congregation to remember them in prayer. Consider having a service of commissioning in worship.

7. Ask children to make thank-you cards for their teachers (or for all the teachers).

8. Have an end-of-the-year celebration (breakfast, parade, skits and plays, music) to honor teachers and classes.

9. Give the teachers a personalized gift (tote bag, mug, pen, notepad) with the name and logo of the church printed on it—or perhaps some of the children's artwork.

10. Ask the governing board of the congregation to make an official statement of gratitude or to write a thank-you note to the teachers.

7 Best Ways to Invite

1. *Begin with an email message.* Send the potential teacher an email message that lays the groundwork for your request. Include why you think the person would be a good teacher for the specific opportunity you are offering. Ask her/him not to respond just yet, and invite her/him to meet with you for further conversation.

2. *One to one, face-to-face.* Make an appointment—to get a cup of coffee or share a homemade dessert—and sit down face-to-face with the potential teacher.

3. *Fellowship and food.* Invite potential teachers/leaders to join some carefully chosen, enthusiastic teachers for dinner. Be up front about the purpose of the invitation. Prepare a list of openings in the educational program on a large sheet of newsprint. After supper, ask the current teachers to say a sentence or two about their experience in the program. Display the list of openings and ask for questions about them. Keep this event light and fun! You may be surprised how many people will volunteer for teaching opportunities. People will often ask someone else to sign up with them at an event like this.

4. *Self-selection.* In late winter to early spring, invite current teachers to complete an evaluation form regarding the education program and their part in it. Include a sentence asking teachers if they are willing to teach the next year. Ask them to indicate which age group they would like to teach. Encourage them to identify people they would like to have as part of a teaching team with them. Follow up with those who do not return their evaluations. Some veteran teachers may assume you know they want to continue—ask them every time anyway.

5. *Month-by-month teaching teams.* In some congregations that are rebuilding an education program or have limited numbers of people willing and able to teach, month-by-month teaching teams might be the second-best option (second-best to having a consistent teaching team for a whole year or season). For example, one teaching team might be responsible for the multiaged church school session for a month or two, then the next team, and so forth throughout the year. While it's not ideal (because of limited opportunities for relationship building with learners), it can work successfully. In this case, inviting the teams to meet for planning and helping them with the transition from one team to the next can make this a satisfying arrangement.

6. *Student referrals (and invitations!).* Visit the classes to ask for input from the participants: who would they recommend to teach their classes? For example, youth know which adults are "cool," which grown-ups they feel comfortable with. In some contexts, it works well to involve the participants in issuing the invitation (particularly true for youth classes; if youth do this, be sure to follow up with the specifics).

7. *Teacher recommendations or requests.* When part of a teaching team is in place, it is often helpful to ask continuing teachers on the team whom they would like to have join them. It is a strong vote of confidence and very persuasive to be told that the people on the second-grade teaching team want you to be the third member of their team!

7 Worst Ways to Invite

1. *General (generic!) announcements, whether from the pulpit or in the bulletin.* "The Christian education committee is in the process of recruiting teachers for next year. If you are willing to teach, call Sister CE Chair at 555-5555."

2. *Using guilt.* "We've never asked you to teach at vacation Bible school because we know you teach fourth graders all day, but VBS is in July, and our regular teachers need a break. You'll be on summer vacation, though, with lots of time to rest before VBS even starts. Shall I put you down to teach?"

3. *False advertising and downplaying expectations.* "Teaching won't take any time at all. We'll put you on a team with other parents so you won't have to do much preparation or even be there every week. It's easy!"

4. *Asking on short notice.* "I know it's August and you're a busy person, but it's never too late to ask, right? Sunday school begins in two weeks. Would you be willing to buy the supplies for the classrooms?"

5. *Recruiting strangers and friends of members.* "Hello. I'm Sister CE Chair from First Baptist Church. I heard from Jean that you are interested in joining our church. The best way to get to know people is by getting involved! Can I sign you up to teach in the afterschool program?"

6. *Expecting to be turned down.* "I know you have never done this before and you probably don't even want to, but since you have a first grader, I thought you might consider teaching her Sunday school class."

7. *The bottom of the barrel.* "You are our last hope. Everyone else has said no, but I'm sure you won't do that. Would you be in charge of finding cooks for the youth suppers on Sunday nights?"

APPENDIX N

10 Terrific Ways to Support Teachers All Year Long

1. Support teachers with school-aged children by being proactive about their need for time away with their families. Be proactive by offering to combine classes or secure substitute teachers for weekends when teachers and their families are more likely to be out of town (pay special attention to Christmas break, spring break, other three-day school holiday weekends).

2. Put up a bulletin board displaying pictures of teachers (with names, especially in a larger or more transient congregation).

3. Before every class, check the classrooms to make sure the space is ready (chairs in place, trash emptied, supplies stored where expected and restocked as necessary, etc.). This is particularly important if the space is used by multiple groups during the day or throughout the week.

4. Recognize the contributions of teachers/leaders in worship (litanies, sermons) and other special events (church picnics, family night suppers). Pray for them specifically in the pastoral prayer from time to time. Notes or email messages of thanks are excellent!

5. Provide special permanent name tags for teachers that identify them as a teacher in the educational program of the congregation. Make sure to have extra name tags for substitutes.

6. Provide coffee/juice/snacks for teachers the hour before class begins in a location where the resource person is available for last-minute questions and needs.

7. Be available after class to listen for joys and concerns generated in class. If appropriate, share these with the pastor and others who

volunteer to pray for participants in the educational ministries. Check in with each teacher on a regular basis regarding participants' joys and concerns.

8. Pay attention to joys or concerns in the lives of teachers. Share words of celebration or support, and offer tangible assistance where appropriate.

9. Ask teachers what would make their work more enjoyable, and then advocate for things they need with congregational leadership.

10. Process reimbursement requests promptly and/or offer to purchase supplies for teachers so they don't have to use their own personal resources and wait for reimbursement. Keep a well-stocked supply closet of common but more infrequently used supplies that aren't kept in classrooms. Provide teachers with an updated inventory of the supply closet (monthly or quarterly).

20 Ways to Support Christian Education without Being in the Classroom

1. Provide snacks for class participants.

2. Gather the supplies and do the preparation needed for activities so that they can be undertaken easily and quickly by teachers during classes.

3. Check and set up the classrooms (clean furniture, set chairs at the tables, check basic supplies, make simple repairs, note repair/replacement needs for trustee consideration).

4. Organize the supply closet and update the inventory list for teachers.

5. Organize the resource room or church library and update the inventory list for teachers.

6. Make photocopies (especially helpful the hour before class).

7. Offer to sit with children of teachers during worship.

8. Design and/or offer to put up bulletin boards.

9. Set up the email group for class participants.

10. Email class members with information about future classes.

11. Respond to bulletin/newsletter announcements about particular needs for craft items.

12. Write a feature story about a teacher column for the newsletter each month (interview the teacher, take the picture, write the article).

13. Get books from the library for children's classes that correspond to the lesson theme.

14. Be the delivery/collection person for snacks, offering, attendance sheets, etc.

15. Set up and maintain records (names, addresses, phone numbers,

attendance, etc.).

16. Organize, prepare, and deliver simple gifts to express gratitude to teachers/leaders.

17. Send birthday cards to all the class participants; help with other correspondence.

18. Assist in the collection of special supplies (yogurt lids, empty two-liter bottles, egg cartons, empty toilet paper or paper towel tubes, strawberry baskets), as necessary.

19. Pray for teachers and participants.

20. Encourage friends to come with you to attend Sunday school or other educational offerings. Be a proponent of lifelong Christian education and practice what you preach.

Sample Form for Meeting Minutes

Minutes of the Christian Education Team
First United Methodist Church

Date: _____

Members attending:
_____
_____

Members excused:
_____

Call to order (time): _____

Minutes of last meeting: _____

Summary of items discussed:
_____
_____

Action items (what, who, when):
_____
_____

Agenda items for next time:

Meeting adjourned (time): _____

Respectfully submitted: _____,
Secretary

Sample Agenda for Christian Education Committee Meeting

Estimated length: 90 minutes

Meeting of the Christian Education Committee
First Congregational Church
[insert date]

First things first [*roughly 15 minutes*]
- Welcome and open with prayer/devotional thought
- Approve agenda (as presented or with additions/corrections)
- Presentation of minutes of last meeting (insert date)
- Report on financial issues (committee budget and expenditures/remaining funds)
- Moment for visioning/check on progress toward strategic plan goals

Review/evaluation of activities since last meeting
(*some examples are below*)
- Children's Christmas play
- Thank-you tea for teachers (Sunday after Christmas—no Sunday school)
- Advent classroom worship centers (LED candles, litanies of candle lighting, etc.)

Appendix Q

Action items from last meeting
(*some examples are below*)
- Curriculum review for next year's Sunday school
- Vacation Bible school planning progress report
- Family intergenerational meal/study nights
- Renovation of Senior Saints' classroom
- Child and Youth Protection Policy review

New action items (*some examples are below*)
- Classroom walk-through to create punch list of items in need of restocking and repairs
- Creation of a "safe children's snacks" list for each classroom and invite donations

Issues to be forwarded to other committees for consideration/action
- Broken sink in women's room on second floor
- Replacement of outlets with child-proof outlet covers in nursery and toddlers' rooms
- Prayer emphasis for congregation during Lent

Sample Christian Education Calendar

This is a sample program calendar for the Christian education ministry team of a midsized congregation. It is intended to be a discussion starter, giving a sense of the flow of the year in one congregation. It is not a recommendation or an indication of what your congregation should do. Each congregation is different and needs to adapt and create programming to meet the needs of its community.

January
- Install newly elected church officers, including Christian education team members
- Winterfest (winter vacation Bible school kind of event— MLK weekend)
- Food drive (all ages) for local food pantry
- Resume six weeks of midweek programming for all ages, followed by Oasis (family time off)
- Plan Lenten Soup and Study series and order Lenten devotional materials for all ages

February
- Confirmation retreat to write personal statements of faith
- Spirituality and spiritual disciplines retreat
- Select and order curriculum for vacation Bible school
- Review curriculum in use in Sunday school and make curriculum choices for next program year

March
- Lenten Soup and Study series begins
- Recruit teachers/leaders for vacation Bible school
- Spring break intergenerational service trip/event

April
- Recruit teachers (two weeks at a time)/order curriculum for Summer One-Room Sunday School
- Easter Eggstravaganza (Easter egg hunt and family craft event)
- Promote denominational summer camp and invite applications for summer camp scholarships

May
- Confirmation service
- Vacation Bible school teacher training event
- Celebrate graduates at all levels
- Publicly thank teachers in worship and with teacher appreciation luncheon following

June
- Birthday of the Church Pentecost party
- Summer One-Room Sunday School starts
- Intergenerational summer pool party
- Begin recruiting Sunday school and midweek programming leaders/teachers for program year

July
- July Jubilee intergenerational learning week (incorporating vacation Bible school)
- Vacation Bible school

August
- Church picnic and outdoor worship service
- Teacher orientation/training event for all teachers who will begin in September
- Blessing of Backpacks for students, teachers, and others involved in public, private, or homeschool

September
- Rally Day family festival and block party
- Commission and dedicate teachers assuming roles in the church
- Program year begins—Sunday school resumes
- Six-week midweek programming blocks resume, followed by Oasis (family time off)

October
- Confirmation retreat for confirmands new to the program (two-year program in seventh and eighth grades)
- Present Bibles to third graders
- Teacher training meeting
- Planning for Advent devotional materials (order) and Advent study events or series

November
- Teacher training meeting/Advent insights and ideas
- Gratitude Night intergenerational dinner

December
- Family Advent supper and learning night
- Children's Christmas Program—Do-It-Yourself Pageant
- Family-friendly early Christmas Eve worship service

Ongoing
- Acolyte training for children turning nine years old (bimonthly)
- Welcome party for families baptizing children
  (cake/coffee reception after worship)
- Parents Club dinner with topic/childcare for parents of
  nursery-aged and toddler children
- Collect picture book donations in outdoor drop-off bin for
  nearby schools with limited resources

Multiple Intelligences Overview

Teaching Suggestions Drawn from Multiple Intelligence Theory
The goal of this appendix is utilize Multiple Intelligences as a rubric for rounding out teaching approaches. This effort moves outside of Gardner's theory of multiple intelligences, which identifies each intelligence with particular content, as he explains in "Reflections On Multiple Intelligences" (http://ocw.metu.edu.tr/pluginfile.php/9275/mod_resource/content/1/Myths.pdf):

> In contrast [to learning style], an intelligence is a capacity, with its component processes, that is geared to a specific content in the world (such as musical sounds or spatial patterns). [For example] interpersonal intelligence has to do with understanding other people, but it is often distorted as a license for cooperative learning.

MI theory does offer the impetus to teach important subjects in a variety of ways. Most teachers lean toward teaching in the ways that they learn best, a tendency that probably does not meet the needs of all learners. Using the intelligences as a rubric for exploring different approaches to educational content and activities is one way that we can expand our teaching practices to meet the needs of diverse learners.

1. Interpersonal—interaction with others, cooperation, and discussion
2. Intrapersonal—introspection and self-reflection activities

3. Visual/spatial—visualizing or use of imagination

4. Verbal/linguistic—language, words, and stories

5. Logical/mathematical—abstract reasoning, logic, and critical thinking

6. Bodily/kinesthetic—muscular movement, dance, and other physical activity

7. Musical/rhythmic—sounds, rhythms, and combinations or progressions

8. Naturalistic—exploration of living things and the natural world

9. Existential—considering ultimate life issues, pondering deep questions

Readers who are interested in learning styles or who want to learn more about the distinction between Multiple Intelligence theory and learning styles can download "Teaching with Respect for Diverse Learning Styles," Workshop 702 on the American Baptist Home Mission Societies website at http://www.nationalministries.org/resources.

Sample Evaluation for Teachers

Thank you for your willingness to share your opinions and evaluative comments as we approach the end of the Sunday school program year. Your input is crucial to our ongoing improvement and effectiveness. When completed, please return this evaluation to the church office!

	Not at all				Very well
The invitation to teach:					
provided sufficient information	1	2	3	4	5
honored my talents and time	1	2	3	4	5
inspired me to do my best	1	2	3	4	5
The room in which I taught:					
was maintained appropriately	1	2	3	4	5
had appropriate/comfortable furnishings	1	2	3	4	5
was stocked with the supplies I needed	1	2	3	4	5
The printed resources:					
were easy to use	1	2	3	4	5
inspired creativity and questions	1	2	3	4	5
attended to multiple intelligences	1	2	3	4	5
made me want to teach	1	2	3	4	5

	Not at all				Very well
The support I received throughout the year:					
helped me feel part of a team	1	2	3	4	5
provided special supplies I needed	1	2	3	4	5
equipped me to use the room and AV	1	2	3	4	5
made me feel appreciated	1	2	3	4	5

Ongoing teacher training/continuing education:

	Not at all				Very well
helped equip me to be a better teacher	1	2	3	4	5
was scheduled conveniently/ honored my time	1	2	3	4	5
addressed questions/raised more questions	1	2	3	4	5
inspired me to be a better teacher	1	2	3	4	5

Something I really enjoyed about teaching this year was:

Something that challenged me about teaching this year was:

With regard to its educational ministry, I'd really like to see our church:

I wish:

I would be willing to consider teaching again:
yes _____   no _____   Call me in a few weeks _____

Please explain:

Name _____ Date _____

APPENDIX U

Sample Invitation Script

A printed script can be exceptionally helpful in making calls to invite teachers into service, but no script can substitute for the genuine and heartfelt words of a dear friend and church member who has come to earn love and respect. Thus, please understand this sample is not "magic" in any way. Use it as a sample from which to create your own invitation script.

When the invitation will take place in several steps, including an introductory meeting:

Hello, is this (name of invitee)? This is (insert your name here), and I'm calling on behalf of the Christian education ministry team at (insert name of church here) Church. Do you have a few minutes to talk? Is now a good time?

Great! Well, I'm calling with an invitation we would like you to consider. It's an invitation to teach as part of our Christian education ministry team. Before we get to a specific invitation to teach a particular age group, I'd like to invite you to a brief meeting after church next Sunday where we can take some time to get to know each other better, and where you can hear more about our church's education ministry. We believe it's important for you to understand what's expected if you choose to teach, what resources and training will be provided, how you will be supported in your work, and who to contact with questions. This meeting will help to answer all those questions and any others you may have. Would you be willing to spend an hour next Sunday after worship learning more about this opportunity?

Wonderful! The meeting will be held next Sunday, (insert date and time), in the (insert location) room at church. There will be refreshments provided. Would it be helpful if I sent a reminder email (or called you to remind you) later in the week? Thank you so much for your time today. See you next Sunday!

When the invitation takes place in person:

Thanks so much for taking a few minutes to meet with me today! As you know, I serve on the Christian education ministry team at (insert name of church here) Church. Today it is my pleasure to invite you, on behalf of the team, to consider an important role as teacher for the (insert name of class here). Our team feels that your gifts for teaching, administration, and discernment equip you well for this task.

Before you answer, I believe it is important for you to know that you wouldn't be alone in this task. As the Christian education ministry team, we would be walking with you all year long. A printed resource is provided for you, and we are planning a training event to equip all of our teachers in using this resource as well as the many supplemental resources our Christian education library offers. We plan quarterly continuing education events that are designed as ongoing learning and growth opportunities for teachers and other interested members of the congregation. Your classroom is equipped with basic supplies, and our supply closet is available to you, as well. And we will work with you to ensure that a substitute teacher is available when you are unable to teach. All of this will be spelled out in greater detail at our first teacher meeting on (date/time) at (location).

Would you be willing to prayerfully consider serving in this way?